NO MORE COMRADES

Finally, Nagy appears. "Comrades!" he begins, but the crowd interrupts him with a roar: "There are no more comrades! We are all Hungarians!"

PARLIAMENT SQUARE, BUDAPEST,

October 23, 1956

NO MORE COMRADES

by

ANDOR HELLER

Chicago **HENRY REGNERY COMPANY** *1957*

CONTENTS

NO MORE COMRADES

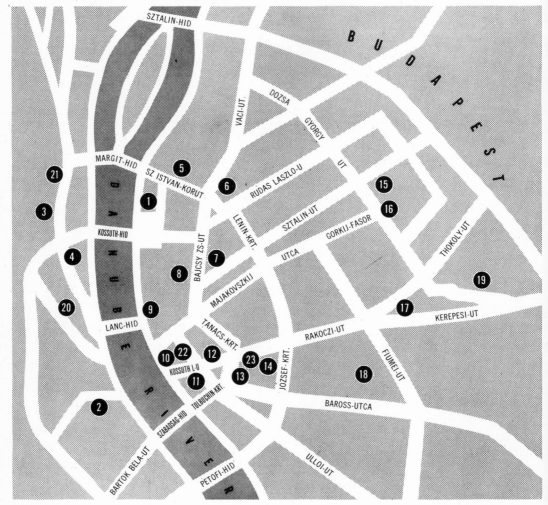

From the start of the Freedom Revolution on October 23, I had been on the streets of Budapest day and night, taking pictures of events as they happened.

CHAPTER 1

MISSION

ON THE MORNING of October 30, 1956, two telegrams were delivered to M.T.I., the official Hungarian news agency, where I worked as a staff photographer. They came from press services in London and Paris. Both urgently begged M.T.I. to send photographs of Hungary's week-old Freedom Revolution.

The woman in charge, an old-line Communist, held the messages in trembling hands. She could hear the tanks now in the hands of the Freedom Fighters—the new national army—rumbling down Tanacs Boulevard to press the fight against the remaining Russians.

Our Comrade Chief—perhaps out of fear, perhaps to get credit in case the patriots won—turned to me and said:

"I wish I could send some pictures to London, but unfortunately no mails are going out at present."

That same morning the M.T.I. staff elected a revolutionary council, following the example of the workers in factories and shops throughout the country. I was chosen chairman. We had already discussed how we could get pictures of our Freedom Revolution out to the free world. We wanted people everywhere to learn about our nation's fight

I was issued a diplomatic passport—Passport No. 1 of the Hungarian revolutionary government. I was assigned the mission: "to use every means possible to tell the people of the world the truth. . . ."

to free our land from Russian control. We also wanted the world to know the truth about the crimes of the Red Army and of the A.V.H.—the sinister State Security Police, modeled after Russia's M.V.D. At the moment we were blocked by the fact that postal connections with the West had been broken.

I therefore proposed to take the pictures out into the free world myself.

I was not a Communist, but I had managed to get a job with M.T.I. because of my training as a professional photographer. From the start of the Freedom Revolution on October 23, I had been on the streets of Budapest day and night, taking pictures of events as they happened. I had three hundred picture negatives, and I was determined to get them to Vienna and from there to every country in the free world.

The next day, October 31, I went to the Ministry of Foreign Affairs, which was controlled by a revolutionary committee. I explained my plan, and showed some of the pictures that I wanted to carry out. One of my childhood friends was a member of the committee, and vouched for me.

I was issued a diplomatic passport—Passport No. 1 of the Hungarian revolutionary government. I was assigned the mission: "to use every means possible to tell the people of the world the truth about the Hungarian Freedom Revolution." I was also instructed to observe developments at the Hungarian Legation in Vienna, and to report back by telephone.

As I left the Ministry I saw the Russian tanks leaving Budapest. Though the fighting was not over, everyone rejoiced. We felt that we had won a great victory, and that the rule of Russian-controlled Communism was coming to an end.

It was noon, and I could hear machine-gun fire. I went to the Austrian Legation to get my visa. When the officials there learned that I was going to drive to Vienna, they asked me to take along an Austrian girl. I agreed, and said we would start in an hour.

Another woman was sitting there listening to us. She started crying, and asked: "Will you take me too?" She had come from Temesvar in Rumania, hoping to escape to Vienna, and from there to join her parents. They had been allowed to emigrate to Israel, but the Rumanian Communist government had refused to let her have a passport to go with them. Since she had no passport, the Austrian Legation could not give her a visa. But her voice was desperate, and I said she could come along.

I hurried home for a briefcase to carry my pictures. I said goodbye to my family, saying that I would be back home in three or four days. With the two fleeing women, I started the drive to Vienna in a 1947 Austin.

There was lots of traffic on the road. Many trucks were headed for the border to pick up medicine and food that had been sent by the free world. But there was a tense silence in the car. The two women were huddled in the back seat listening to the noise of the distant machine-gun fire.

6

Just after leaving the city of Komarom, our car was fired on by Russian soldiers. Luckily their aim was bad, and they hit nothing but the fenders. About half way to the border, in the town of Gyor, we were stopped by Freedom Fighters, who asked for our identification. When I showed them my new diplomatic passport and told them my mission, they immediately cleared the road for us. Before reaching the Austrian border we were stopped seven more times by Freedom Fighters. Apparently the Russians and the A.V.H. agents had been pushed out of this area; at any rate, we saw no signs of either.

We reached Vienna at 9:30 that night (October 31). After dropping off my passengers, I went at once to the Hungarian Legation and identified myself. The Minister and his entire staff were upset by my arrival. They knew that Hungarian patriots were now in control of our country, and that Communists and their collaborators would soon lose their government posts.

On Saturday, November 3, I telephoned the Foreign Ministry in Budapest by a direct line from the Hungarian Legation in Vienna. I reported on the arrangements made for distributing the pictures and on other matters connected with our fight for freedom and national independence. I also made a complete report on the situation as I saw it in the Legation. I was told to remain in Vienna for a few more days and to keep my eyes and ears open.

As the free world knows, the Red Army, with artillery, infantry and hundreds of tanks, again attacked Budapest in the early morning hours of November 4. The Hungarian

Freedom Fighters and the whole city rose as one man against this new invasion. All the unbelievable cruelty of the Communist-led Russians came down on the Hungarian people. All communications with the outside world were broken.

My mission to the free world thus became more vital than ever. I must stay on in the free world to tell the story of our Freedom Revolution, and how it had come about. I must try to explain the struggle of the Hungarian nation, and warn all people how Russian Communism threatens the freedom and independence of every nation and all the people of the world.

A few days later I was on my way to the United States of America to begin by telling our story before a Committee of the United States Senate. In order not to endanger the lives of my wife and child, who were still in Hungary, I appeared masked and under the name of Arpad Hazafi. They have since then found refuge in the United States, so that it is possible for me to reveal my true identity and the nature of my mission to the free world.

This book is dedicated to all those heroes, of every age and walk of life, who died in Hungary for the cause of human freedom, and to the unconquerable spirit of the Hungarian nation that in the end will be victorious over the Russian Communists who now, by armed force and terror, occupy my country.

CHAPTER 2

THE
FREEDOM REVOLUTION

I SAW FREEDOM rise from the ashes of Communism in Hungary: a freedom that flickered and then blazed before it was beaten down—but not extinguished—by masses of Russian tanks and troops.

I saw young students, who had known nothing but a life under Communist and Russian control, die for a freedom about which they had only heard from others or from their own hearts.

I saw workers, who had been pushed to the limit of endurance by their hopeless existence under Communism, lay down their tools and take up arms in a desperate bid to win back freedom for our country.

I saw a girl of fourteen blow up a Russian tank, and grandmothers walk up to Russian cannons.

I watched a whole nation—old and young, men and women, artists and engineers and doctors, clerks and peasants and factory workers—become heroes overnight as they rose up in history's first successful revolt against Communism.

With my own eyes and my camera's eye, I saw Hungary's Freedom Revolution.

9

Tuesday, October 23, 1956

No Hungarian will forget this day.

Yesterday the students held meetings at the Universities. In the afternoon they demonstrated silently before the Polish Embassy, in sympathy with the Poles who were demanding a liberalized regime and more independence from Moscow.

The papers and radio, under Party Secretary Erno Gero's orders, don't carry a line about it, but we all know that there will be a student demonstration this afternoon at the Monument in Petofi* Square, on the east bank of the Danube. In spite of the cold and fog, students are on the streets early in the morning, marching and singing. No one shows up for classes at the universities. After a decade of Communist control over our country, we are going to show our feelings spontaneously, in our own way—something never allowed under Communist rules.

The students carry signs with slogans that until now we have never dared express except to members of our own family—and not in every family. The slogans read:

> RUSSIANS GO HOME!
> LET HUNGARY BE INDEPENDENT!
> BRING RAKOSI TO JUSTICE!
> WE WANT A NEW LEADERSHIP!
> SOLIDARITY WITH THE POLISH PEOPLE!
> WE TRUST IMRE NAGY—BRING IMRE NAGY
>   INTO THE GOVERNMENT!

* Petofi was the famous 19-century poet of Hungary's struggle for independence.

In spite of the cold and fog, students are on the streets early in the morning, marching and singing.

The walls of Budapest are plastered with leaflets put up by the students during the night. They list the fourteen demands adopted at the stormy meetings held at the universities:

1. Withdrawal of all Soviet troops from Hungary.

2. Complete economic and political equality with the Soviet Union, with no interference in Hungary's internal affairs.

3. Publication of Hungary's trade agreements, and a public report on Hungary's reparations payments to the U.S.S.R.

4. Information on Hungary's uranium resources, their exploitation, and the concessions given to the U.S.S.R.

5. The calling of a Hungarian Communist Party congress to elect a new leadership.

6. Reorganization of the government, with Imre Nagy as Premier.*

7. A public trial of Mihaly Farkas and Matyas Rakosi.†

8. A secret general multi-party election.

9. The reorganization of Hungary's economy on the basis of her actual resources.

* Imre Nagy, who had been expelled from the Party in April 1955 for "anti-Marxist nationalist leanings and right-wing deviationism," was believed to stand for greater independence from Moscow, political liberalization, and an economic policy designed to raise Hungarian living standards. He had been readmitted to the Party in August 1956.

† Farkas had been Minister of Defense and Rakosi Party Secretary, until July 1956, when both were ousted as notorious Stalinists.

10. Revision of the workers' output quotas, and recognition of the right to strike.

11. Revision of the system of compulsory agricultural quotas.

12. Equal rights for individual farmers and cooperative members.

13. Restoration of Hungary's traditional national emblem and the traditional Hungarian army uniforms.*

14. Destruction of the giant statue of Stalin.†

During the morning a radio announcement from the Ministry of Interior bans all public meetings and demonstrations "until further notice," and word is sent to the universities that the student demonstrations cannot be held. At that moment the students decide that the will to freedom is greater than the fear of the A.V.H.—the Russian-controlled Hungarian secret police. The meeting will be held!

Peter Kucka, the Communist poet who was silenced by the Rakosi government because of his public criticisms, answers for the students, and states that the demonstration will take place at 3 P.M. as scheduled. At 2 P.M., the Minister of the Interior, to head off the open flouting of his authority, gives way. He sends word to the thousands of students gathered at the Technological University that the regime has decided "to permit" the demonstration. He warns the stu-

* Under the Communist regime the Hungarian army had been using a Russian-type uniform.

† Later a 15th, and still later a 16th, point were added: 15. Solidarity with the national movement in Poland. 16. Dissolution of the A.V.H.

Six abreast, we march across the Chain Bridge over the Danube to the Buda (left) side of the city.

dents against "excesses," and against "criticism of the government."

As representative of the Hungarian news agency (M.T.I.) I have been on the streets since morning with my camera. In the early afternoon I join the student crowds at Petofi Square and Museum Boulevard, on the Pest side of the city —the right bank of the Danube.

As we march the few blocks to the Petofi Monument, our group grows in size every minute. More and more students join us and then some of the bystanders on the sidewalks, who have been waving and cheering, also begin to get in line.

At 3 P.M. there are 25,000 of us at the Petofi Monument. We weep as Imre Sinkovits, a young actor, declaims the *Nemzeti Dal* ("National Song"), Sandor Petofi's ode to Hungary and our 1848 "freedom revolution." With tears in our eyes, we repeat the refrain with Sinkovits:

"Eskuszunk, eskuszunk, hogy rabok tovabb nem leszunk."

("We swear, we swear, we will no longer remain slaves.")

The student voices are tense with feeling. No policeman or Communist official is in sight. The young people are keeping order on their own.

The moving and peaceful demonstration at the Petofi Monument ends, but we have not had enough of the unaccustomed taste of free expression. Six abreast, we march across the Chain Bridge over the Danube to the Buda (left) side of the city. We head for the statue of Joseph Bem, the Polish general who in 1848 led the Hungarian patriot army against the Hapsburg rulers, and then against the

By the time we arrive at the Bem statue we have swelled to some 60,000.

Peter Veres, the head of the Hungarian Writers' Federation, reads the Hungarian writers' demands for more freedom—many of them the same as those in the fourteen points of the students.

Russian troops who finally crushed that earlier revolt.

By the time we arrive at the Bem statue we have swelled to some 60,000. Someone grabs a Hungarian flag and cuts out the hated hammer and sickle that the Communists had placed at its center.

One after another of the purified Hungarian flags appear. Suddenly someone remembers to put the old Kossuth* coat-of-arms on the flag, in place of the Communist emblem.

We have created a new flag of freedom!

Meantime we all sing the Szozat *Appeal to the Nation,* and the *Hungarian National Hymn* that begins "God Bless the Magyar"—both of which had been banned under the Communist rule.

We cannot get enough. The actor Ferenc Bessenyei recites the *National Song* again, and follows once more with *Appeal to the Nation.* Peter Veres, the head of the Hungarian Writers' Federation, leaps to the top of a car equipped with a loudspeaker. He reads the Hungarian writers' demands for more freedom—many of them the same as those in the fourteen points of the students.

The day is ending. We begin to march toward the Parliament Building. The crowds are peaceful, marching in orderly lines. We carry the new Hungarian flag.

As we march we are joined by workers leaving their jobs. By the time we arrive in Kossuth Lajos Square there are at least 150,000 of us, in front of the Parliament Building. On the square, all traffic stops.

* Louis (Lajos) Kossuth was the great Hungarian hero of the 1848 Revolution.

Someone grabs a Hungarian flag and cuts out the hated hammer and sickle that the Communists had placed at its center.

By the time we
arrive at Kossuth
Lajos Square there
are at least 150,000
of us, in front of the
Parliament Building.

Although still orderly, the crowd begins demanding the appearance of Imre Nagy—the only prominent Communist for whom the people still have some personal feeling.

Suddenly, in the twilight, the Red Star on top of the Parliament Building—the symbol of Moscow's control over our country—is lighted. The crowd begins to roar, "Put out the Red Star!" And as suddenly as it came on, the light is turned off.

We hear a weak voice from the balcony in front of the building: "Give us twenty minutes. Comrade Nagy is on his way, and the loudspeaker is being set up."

It gets darker. Various cars with loudspeakers are among the crowd, but we are not sure whether they are manned by friends or by Communists, so we don't let them talk.

The twenty minutes are up, and there takes place a typical Communist trick. Instead of the promised appearance of Nagy—which might have quieted everything down—the street lights in Kossuth Square are abruptly turned out. One hundred and fifty thousand people stand together in the dark.

Suddenly everyone makes torches of newspapers, and lights them. It is a marvelous spectacle—ten thousand torches burning in the Square before the Parliament Building.

Nagy still has not shown up, and we begin to get impatient. "Let's go to Stalin Square," someone shouts, "and not to recite poems. Let's pull down Stalin's statue."

But finally, Imre Nagy appears on the balcony. "Comrades!" he begins, but the crowd interrupts him with a roar:

But finally, Imre Nagy appears on the balcony. "Comrades!" he begins, but the crowd interrupts him with a roar. "There are no more comrades! We are all Hungarians!"

"There are no more comrades! We are all Hungarians!"

The crowd is now cold toward Nagy, whom we have formerly trusted. First, he is two hours late. Then he addresses us by the hated Communist term, "Comrade." Someone says, "Let's have some light on Imre Nagy," and three flashlights shine on his face as he speaks.

While Nagy is calming us and saying that the students' and workers' demands are justified, another voice is speaking over Radio Budapest—the voice of a man hated by the entire Hungarian nation: Erno Gero, Secretary and boss of the Hungarian Communist Party. Gero says that any rumor that Hungary wants to loosen its "close and friendly ties" with "the glorious Soviet Union" is "a barefaced lie, hostile slander without a grain of truth." He calls the demonstration a "fascist putsch" and the students a "fascist mob and gang of bandits."

Word of Gero's radio speech runs through the crowd. We are enraged. At the very moment that Nagy is speaking to us, Hungary's Communist overlord contradicts what Nagy is saying.

The crowd grows still bigger, and we head for the Stalin statue. Now the demonstration has spread so large that it is going on simultaneously in three places: at the Parliament Building; in Stalin Square, where the crowd is trying to pull down the huge Stalin statue with tractors and ropes; and at the building of Radio Budapest, where part of the crowd has gone to demand the right of patriots to be heard over the air.

I go with the group that heads for Stalin Square. Some of

... the crowd is trying to pull down the huge Stalin statue with tractors and ropes. ...

the workers have got hold of acetylene torches. They and the students are trying to cut down the dictator's twenty-five-foot metal figure. At the edge of the crowd the first Russian tanks appear, but at the moment they are only on-lookers. The crowd pulls hard at the cables that have been attached to the Stalin statue. It leans forward, but is still held by its boots—a symbol, we feel. The cables are now being pulled by tractors, and the men with the torches work feverishly. The statue, though still in one piece, begins to bend at the knees. The crowds burst into cheers.

In the midst of the cheering we hear the ominous report: there has been shooting at Radio Budapest. We start by truck for the Radio building. Looking back from Dozsa Gyorgy Street, we watch the Stalin statue, cut off at the knees, fall to the ground with a thunderous crash.

When we get to the Communist-controlled Radio building in Alexander Brody Street, we find out what has happened. A youth delegation tried to get in the door, in order to have their "14 demands" broadcast over the radio. Without warning, the security police guarding the building opened up on them with tear-gas bombs.

Suddenly shooting breaks out from all sides. The security police—the A.V.H.—are firing into the crowds. In minutes, the streets are strewn with the dying and wounded. News of the A.V.H. attack spreads. All over Budapest the workers and students are battling the hated A.V.H.

The peaceful demonstrations of the youth and the workers have been turned by Communist guns into a revolution for national freedom.

The statue, though still in one piece, begins to bend at the knees. The crowds burst into cheers.

. . . we watch the Stalin statue, cut off at the knees, fall forward to the ground with a thundering crash.

Wednesday, October 24

Our flat is fifteen minutes out from the center of Budapest, at the corner of the road that leads to the town of Szekesfehervar, which is used as a base by the Russian occupation forces. During the night of October 23/24 my wife and I are wakened by metallic sounds we recognize: Russian tanks and armored cars moving by our corner on the way from Szekesfehervar to the center of Budapest.

The street is very slippery, and some of the machines skid as they round the corner. In the morning we look out and see that a tank has smashed three lamp posts.

We learn that heavy fighting has gone on through the night, particularly around the Radio building, the National Museum, the Kilian Barracks, and in the chiefly working-class 8th and 9th city districts.

We hear that at dawn the patriot forces—the Freedom Fighters—had penetrated the Radio building. But the radio facilities are still under the control of Erno Gero and the A.V.H., apparently using auxiliary studios in rock-cellar shelters.

Instructed by Gero, Radio Budapest broadcasts streams of lies that are refuted by one glance into the streets of the city:

"Fascist, reactionary elements have launched an armed attack against our public buildings and have attacked our armed forces. . . . The dastardly armed attacks of counter-revolutionary gangs during the night have created an extremely serious situation. The bandits have penetrated into factories and public buildings. . . ." Well, at least the broad-

They are planting the new Hungarian flags on them, and then heading them toward Kossuth Lajos Square and the Parliament Building.

casts tell us indirectly that the Hungarian patriots and Freedom Fighters are not doing too badly.

Then another typical Communist trick. At 7:15 A.M. Radio Budapest announces that a new government has just been formed with Imre Nagy as Premier. We have won the second of our demands! (The toppling of the Stalin statue was the first.) Then, at 8:00 P.M. the radio declares: "The government was unprepared for these bloody dastardly attacks and therefore applied for help, in accordance with the terms of the Warsaw Treaty, to the Soviet formations stationed in Hungary." Because of the order of the two broadcasts, it looks to most of us as if Imre Nagy had asked for the Soviet intervention. I know, of course, that the tanks I heard must have started toward Budapest early last night, before Nagy had any place in the government, and while the demonstrations were still peaceful. It is another fraud by Erno Gero, who remains as Party Secretary.

During the night scores of Russian tanks have reached the city proper, and linked up with those that we saw yesterday in Stalin Square. But when we gather in the streets this morning—firing had quieted down at the moment—we see that our Freedom Fighters have already captured some of them. They are planting the new Hungarian flags on them, and then heading them toward Kossuth Lajos Square and the Parliament Building.

I rush ahead to the square, which I reach at noon. A sickening sight meets my eyes. The open square is filled with the bodies of wounded and dying. Shocked and terrified survivors tell us what has happened.

A sickening sight
meets my eyes. The
open square is filled
with the bodies of
wounded and dying.

A few minutes before, thousands of unarmed workers and students had· gathered peacefully in the square, before the Parliament Building, to present a petition to the government.

A few minutes before, thousands of unarmed workers and students had gathered peacefully in the square, before the Parliament Building, to present a petition to the government. A few Russian tanks were drawn up carelessly around the edges. Suddenly the A.V.H., stationed on the roof of the Ministry of Agriculture building at the opposite side of the square, fired into the backs of the crowd. The Russians, apparently not sure where the firing was coming from, started shooting into the square from their tanks. An estimated six hundred persons were lying dead or wounded on the pavement. My sixteen-year-old assistant, Peter Gardos, who was there to take photographs, is among those who are dead.

Now the enraged workers, as well as the students, begin to get arms. Some of the weapons are distributed by the Hungarian soldiers at the Kilian and Bem barracks; some are brought by workers from the Matyas Rakosi steel plant on Csepel Island in the Danube, and from the Danuvia munitions factory. Others come from what the Communists used to tell us was a lamp factory—but which we knew turned out munitions for the Communist armies.

By afternoon the quickly organized units of patriot Freedom Fighters are facing the Red Army troops, tanks and armored cars and the A.V.H. all over the city. The official radio cheers us by denouncing "battling groups armed with automatic pistols, machine guns, hand grenades and other weapons."

On the radio Gero and his spokesmen defend the use of Russian troops and says that Hungarians must "welcome our friends and allies with love." A curfew is announced, and a state of emergency together with martial law throughout Hungary. A decree has set up special courts that can pass death sentences against persons found guilty of "rebellion, or possession of arms."

It is rumored that Soviet Deputy Premier Mikoyan and Mikhail Suslov, the Kremlin's expert on the captive nations, have arrived to try to regain control. In a late broadcast, the Communist radio attempts another deception: "More and more factories are starting to work. . . . Restoration of streetcar service. . . . Further bloodshed is senseless. . . . The Government is master of the situation. Let peaceful, constructive work start in as many places as possible, in factories, enterprises and shops."

On my way home I see the National Museum burning, set ablaze by Russian tank fire. At the corner of St. Stephen Road I almost step on the bodies of three unarmed demonstrators murdered by the Russians. On Ulloi Road their tanks and armored cars have blasted a children's hospital.

Thursday, October 25

The government is confused. One hour it declares a curfew and warns everyone to stay off the streets and inside their homes behind locked doors. The next it appeals to everyone to get back to their jobs.

In fact, what has become a general strike has spread and continues uninterrupted. The factories and nearly every office are empty. Schools are closed. Streetcars are at a stand-

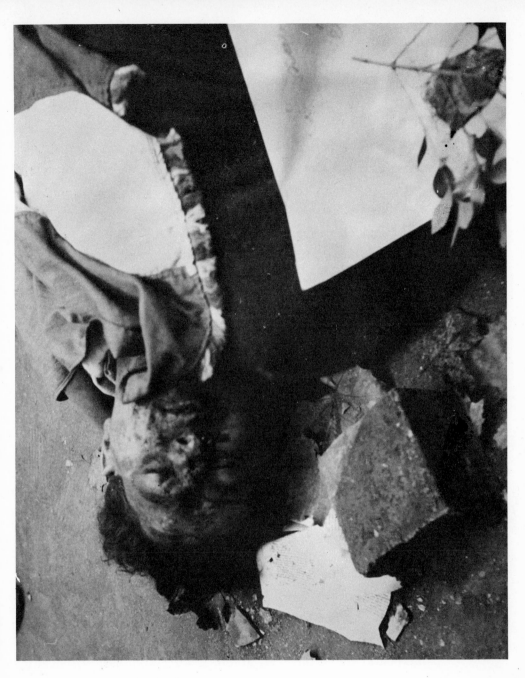

At the corner of St. Stephen Road I almost step on the bodies of three unarmed demonstrators murdered by the Russians.

still. There has been much damage to the power and light equipment.

The radio continues to broadcast government threats of the death penalty on those who continue fighting or who even keep arms. But the authority of the government is vanishing. Today I have seen many Hungarian soldiers tear the Communist badges off their caps and join the demonstrations that are becoming a revolution. We hear that thousands of the soldiers of the Hungarian Army are joining the units of Freedom Fighters, and turning weapons and ammunition over to them.

As I pass the Kilian Zalka Mate barracks, soldiers are passing guns and ammunition through the windows to civilians outside. All over Budapest Freedom Fighters are tearing Red Stars down from the buildings and burning Red flags. They have taken over the building of *Szabad Nep,* the official Communist Party newspaper, and pried the huge Red Star from its top.

Then everyone cheers a radio communique from the Communist Party Politburo: "The Central Committee relieved Comrade Erno Gero of his post of First Secretary. The Central Committee appointed Janos Kadar as First Secretary." The despised Gero is out! Kadar, who had been arrested and imprisoned along with Rajk, and who has the reputation of being an anti-Stalinist, will replace him.

In a radio address, Imre Nagy promises to convene Parliament and to "submit an all-embracing and basic program of reform." He says that the government will begin talks with the Soviet Union "concerning the withdrawal of the

36

All over Budapest
Freedom Fighters
are tearing Red
Stars down from the
buildings and
burning Red Flags.

Soviet forces stationed in Hungary. These talks will be carried out on the basis of equality and national independence between Communist Parties and Socialist countries." But these phrases sound empty to those who are fighting in the streets of Budapest.

Late at night we hear a first broadcast from the first radio station to get into loyal Hungarian hands—in the provincial town of Miskolc. "End the massacre of Hungarians in Budapest," it began. "Do not believe lies. Let them withdraw Soviet troops from Hungary. Strike!"

Friday, October 26

Just after midnight, Radio Miskolc continues its freedom broadcasts. We learn that in Miskolc and the surrounding Borsod County the revolution has been successful without bloodshed. Authority is in the hands of a joint "national committee," formed from the workers' councils. Radio Miskolc declares:

"Our proclamation issued to the workers . . . consists of five points, as follows: 1. We demand that the Soviet Army leave the country immediately; 2. A new Hungarian government; 3. The right of workers to strike; 4. Complete amnesty for Hungarians who have participated in the revolution; 5. As long as these are not fulfilled the people of Borsod County and Greater Miskolc respectively will strike, with the exception of railways, mining, health services, public supply, electric power supply and the press. . . .

"Young workers and students: conduct yourselves in a disciplined manner. . . . Do not commit any provocation or any sabotage. . . . We are able to assert our demands without bloodshed."

It is becoming clear that Budapest is united with the whole country in the struggle for freedom! At Pecs, to the south, after a brief struggle, the radio station has also been taken over and begins broadcasting under revolutionary direction. There is a story that at Pecs a revolutionary government for the entire southern region has been set up.

We hear that the revolution is spreading throughout the nation. There is fighting at Tatabanya, Salgotarjan and Gyor, and apparently some fighting also at Debrecen, Szolnok and Szeged. The entire area between Magyarovar and the frontier town of Hegyeshalom is in our hands. In much of the countryside the revolution is winning without fighting, because there is no one who supports the Communist regime. In some towns where Red Army troops are stationed, they just look the other way when a "revolutionary committee" or "national committee" is set up.

But Budapest is wakened before dawn by tank and artillery fire. The Russian forces have been ordered to carry out a "general attack" on the Freedom Fighters. Radio Budapest declares that the ban of meetings and public gatherings of more than three persons is still in effect and that citizens will be shot on the spot if they appear in the streets with arms. But no one will any longer obey what Radio Budapest orders. The general strike continues. The Freedom Fighters hold their positions. And ordinary citizens show their defiance by gathering on the streets, often right under the muzzles of Red cannon.

39

And ordinary citizens show their defiance by gathering on the streets, often right under the muzzles of Red cannon.

They have ripped up
streetcar tracks to
make tank barriers.

. . . and overturned streetcars and buses at strategic points.

Now they are distributing the food free at street corners; the peasants permit the Freedom Fighters as much as they need.

There is no automobile traffic on the streets today because the Freedom Fighters, helped by unarmed patriots, have built barricades on nearly every street. They have ripped up streetcar tracks to make tank barriers, and overturned streetcars and buses at strategic points. Many streetcars stand motionless, with shattered windows, where their motormen have abandoned them to join the Freedom Revolution.

Food is getting scarce. There are long lines of people waiting at the stores for hours to buy potatoes, milk or a loaf of bread. But there is a bright spot in the food supply.

From the villages around Budapest the peasants have begun to send in carts and trucks with food for the patriots in the city. Much of it has been hidden away from the Communist authorities and the system of compulsory deliveries. Now they are distributing the food free at street corners; the peasants permit the Freedom Fighters as much as they need. The housewives and small children are becoming a supply service for the new patriot army that is rising out of the Freedom Revolution.

Moving around the city today, I have seen many of these free food deliveries. At one corner a bearded peasant and his wife toss out potatoes like balls in a game. In another street, a truck pulls in loaded with fish that were still alive. They throw them out, and many of them slip through fingers to the sidewalk, where they jump around as if just caught.

The curfew is now officially in force from 10 in the morning until 3 in the afternoon, but no one pays attention. The

The Freedom
Fighters are out at
all hours.

I see a Russian armored car fire without any reason at three women and four men passing by—all unarmed.

Freedom Fighters are out at all hours. Others go out to get food, or on other errands, or just to see what is happening.

Some of them are shot. I see a Russian armored car fire without any reason at three women and four men‚passing by—all unarmed. Their bodies still lie in the street as I get away.

In Buda our forces now occupy a number of positions. Workers from the Ganz factory hold Szena Square and Szell Kalman Square. By mid-afternoon, however, the Russians have seized the most important communications points: Margit bridge, the western railroad station, Rakoczi Road, Kossuth Lajos Street.

But we hear today that an entire Hungarian armored regiment, with its tanks, has come over in a body to our side. In fact, almost the entire Hungarian army is swinging behind the nation. Mimeographed leaflets appear on the streets, urging the people to join together "for the liberation of our country from the Russian yoke." Shop windows are plastered with slogans: RUSSIANS GO HOME! A FREE ELECTION WITH U.N. SUPERVISION!

Our youngsters are teaching us the meaning of courage. They build tank barricades out of paving stones. I watched boys and girls of fourteen or fifteen crawl up to Russian tanks and put paving stones in their drive chains. The tank starts, the stone forces the caterpillar tread off the wheels, and the machine is stopped.

The young people have learned about the tanks' blind spots, and how to get close with Molotov cocktails—bottles filled with gasoline and with a fuse of gasoline-soaked rags.

47

But we hear today
that an entire
Hungarian armored
regiment, with its
tanks, has come
over in a body to
our side.

Mimeographed leaflets appear on the streets, urging the people to join together "for the liberation of our country from the Russian yoke."

Shop windows are
plastered with
slogans: RUSSIANS
GO HOME!

A FREE ELECTION
WITH U.N.
SUPERVISION!

They are destroying tanks by the dozens. The gasoline flames force out the Russians, and they are shot from the windows of the surrounding buildings.

The young boys and girls are also fighting with rifles and automatic guns. The weapons, whether from Hungarian army stores or captured in the fighting, are Russian—the Russians are being shot by their own bullets. Today one group of students with a bazooka smashed several Red tanks. And the women are joining, some with weapons, others carrying flags and food and taking care of the wounded.

Russian atrocities continue. I see a combined squad of Russian soldiers and A.V.H. Hungarian traitors firing at plainly marked Red Cross workers, and at trucks, painted with a big Red Cross, which patriot drivers, many of them girls, were using to take the wounded to hospitals. The hospitals in Budapest are filled by now, and many of the wounded must be taken to the villages surrounding our capital.

I also watch Red Army tanks fire at random at houses, on the off chance that a Freedom Fighter might be inside. The fronts of many houses are being smashed open by the cannon fire, so that one can look right into the rooms.

The Red Army throws itself into a bold destruction of property. The Red tanks use church steeples for target practice. Without any reason they knock over light and telephone poles and smash streetcar safety islands.

One of our free radio stations in the provinces reports that at Magyarovar, near the Austrian frontier, Hungarian

Our youngsters are
teaching us the
meaning of courage.
They build tank
barricades out of
paving stones.

The gasoline flames force out the Russians, and they are shot from the windows of the surrounding buildings.

And the women are joining, some with weapons, others carrying flags and food and taking care of the wounded.

Russian atrocities continue.

boys were shot down by Russian soldiers when they climbed on top of a barracks to remove the Red Star.

There is not only too little room for the wounded in Budapest. There is not enough space for the dead. Since the fighting became general it has been impossible to take our dead to the cemeteries which are at the edge of town. We must now use the parks as burial grounds for our fallen heroes.

But today the Freedom Revolution wins a great new victory on another front. The first issues of a free newspaper —*Igazsag* ("Truth")—are printed and rushed quickly to every section of Budapest. It is the first news in a decade that has not been doctored by Communist censors. Other issues of our free newspaper are taken to the villages.

Today in Stalin Square, at the toppled statue, workers and boys have finally managed to behead the fallen dictator. Demonstrators are smashing the hated metal symbol to pieces, and a Hungarian flag flies rakishly from one of its boots.

In the afternoon Radio Budapest broadcasts a declaration by the reorganized Central Committee of the Communist Party. The Committee pledges a new election, negotiations with Moscow, "Correction of past mistakes," a general amnesty, wage increases, and the recognition of the workers' councils that have been elected in the factories.

Tonight, near the Astoria hotel, I am shown the spot where a young woman doctor, who was giving first aid to a wounded young Freedom Fighter, was deliberately shot by a Red tank gunner. Her body was carried away by patriots,

There is not only too little room for the wounded in Budapest. There is not enough space for the dead.

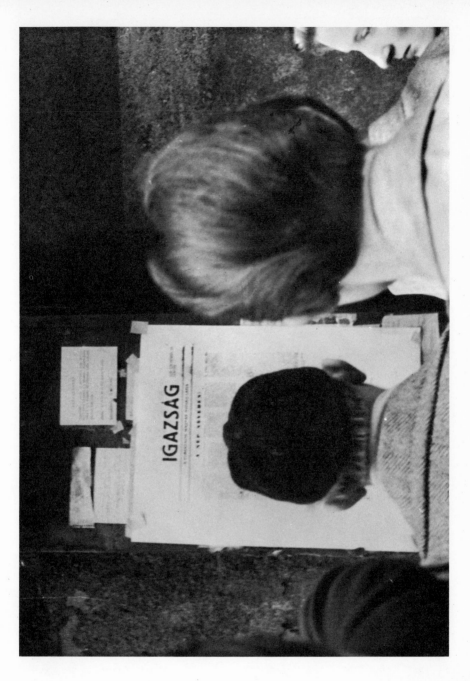

The first issues of a free newspaper—Igazsag ("Truth")—are printed and rushed quickly to every section of Budapest.

We must now use the parks as burial grounds for our fallen heroes.

Other issues of our free newspaper are taken to the villages.

and in its place they left a small white wreath of flowers.

Every house in Budapest now flies the new Hungarian flag—for freedom; and a black flag—for those who gave their lives for freedom. The whole city mourns for the fallen.

Saturday, October 27

There is still heavy fighting in Budapest today. Food is growing scarce, and the general strike continues. There are rumors that Russian tanks are coming from Czechoslovakia to help put down our revolution.

But a curious thing is happening. Hungarians are losing the sense of fear. If a child can blow up a tank, why should anyone be afraid of a tank? As a tank clanks by on the way to a spot where fighting is going on, housewives stroll by arm in arm, and look it over curiously, as if it were an exhibit at a circus. Two minutes after a battle, the sidewalks will be crowded with people inspecting a tank that has been put out of action.

But it is just the opposite with the Russians. They are getting frightened. And they are hungry. They can't get food from the Hungarian peasants, and their own supply systems seem to have broken down. The narrow streets of the old parts of town are not healthy for a tank at night, and the soldiers would be shot if they got out of their machines. So most of the tanks withdraw at night from the center of town into the suburbs.

We still don't know just what to think about Nagy, our new Premier. Today Radio Budapest announced that a new

. . . I am shown the spot where a young woman doctor, who was giving first aid to a wounded young Freedom Fighter, was deliberately shot by a Red tank gunner.

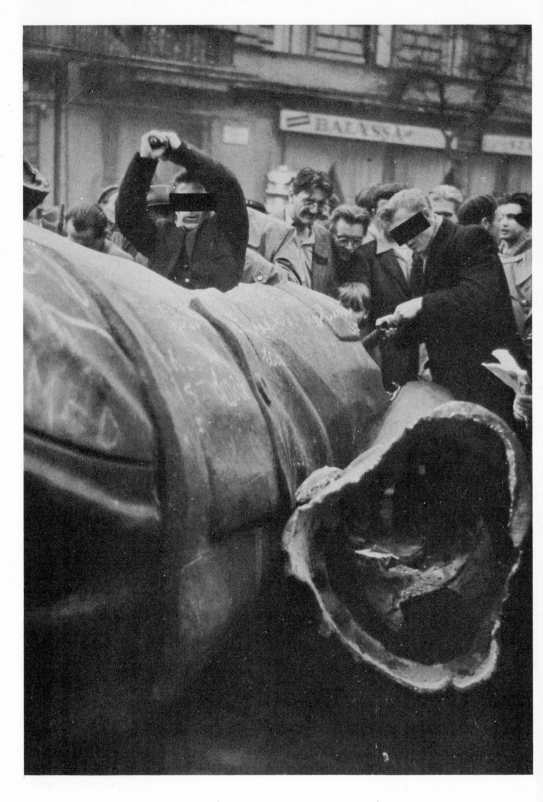

Demonstrators are smashing the hated metal symbol to pieces. . . .

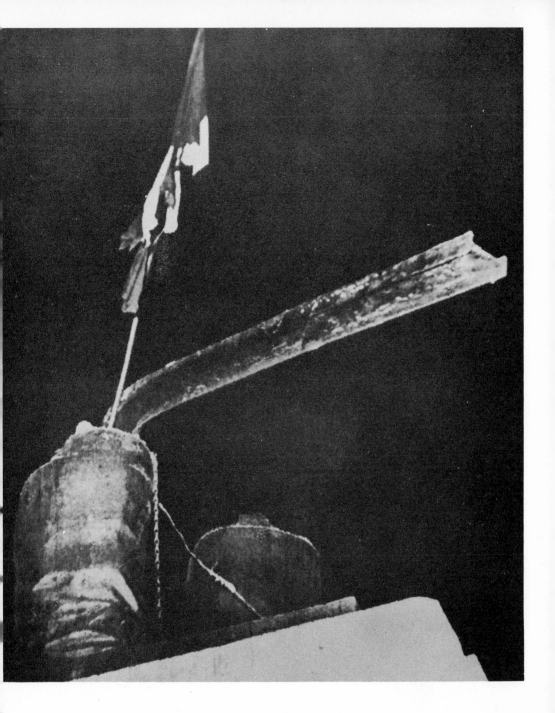

. . . and a Hungarian flag flies rakishly from one of its boots.

But there is a grim report that at Magyarovar, only ten miles from the Austrian border, Red soldiers massacred eighty-five peasants, including women and children.

government has been formed, with two non-Communists given important posts: Zoltan Tildy as Minister of State and Bela Kovacs as Minister of Agriculture. Both belong to the Smallholders Party, long outlawed by the Communists. But we hear from the free radio at Pecs that Kovacs is not in Budapest but in Pecs, with the revolutionary government that has been formed there.

Therefore we do not know what to believe about another announcement attributed to Nagy: that the Russian troops will be out of the country by New Year's Day. Meanwhile a delegation from the workers' councils has presented a list of twenty-one demands to the Premier.

We know that we can trust the radio stations controlled by the patriot forces better than Radio Budapest, which is still under Communist direction. The list of free radio stations is growing daily. It now includes Miskolc, Pecs, Gyor, Magyarovar, and Szombathely.

This afternoon, over Radio Free Miskolc, the workers' council of Borsod County greets the new government, but announces that they will continue their strike until "our demands and, above all, the one concerning withdrawal of Soviet troops, are fulfilled."

Radio Free Miskolc continues: "For two days the city of Miskolc has been under the leadership of the workers' council and the students' parliament. The workers' council has taken over control of the garrison and the police. . . ." Radio Free Pecs reports complete agreement between the local army units and the workers.

From other broadcasts and from leaflets brought into

Two minutes after a battle, the sidewalks will be crowded with people inspecting a tank that has been put out of action.

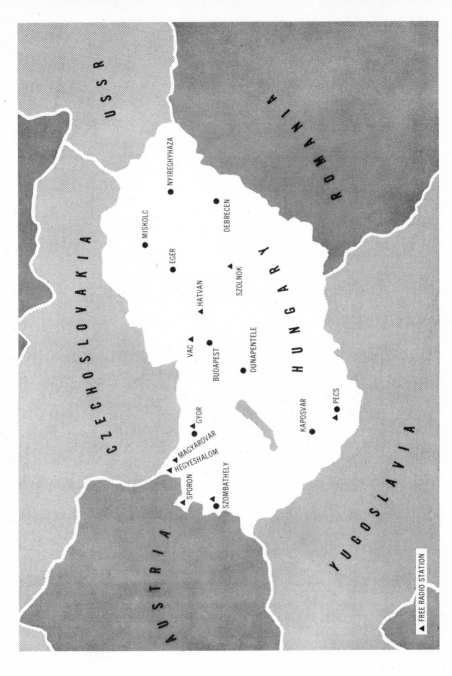

USSR

CZECHOSLOVAKIA

ROMANIA

● MISKOLC

● NYIREGHYHAZA

● EGER

● DEBRECEN

▲ HATVAN

▲ SZOLNOK

H U N G A R Y

VAC ▲

● BUDAPEST

DUNAPENTELE

GYOR ▲

▲ PECS

▲ MAGYAROVAR

KAPOSVAR ●

▲ HEGYESHALOM

▲ SPORON

SZOMBATHELY

AUSTRIA

YUGOSLAVIA

▲ FREE RADIO STATION

We know that we can trust the radio stations controlled by the patriot forces better than Radio Budapest, which is still under Communist direction. The list of free radio stations is growing daily.

Budapest, we learn that Vac, Hatvan and Szolnok have pro-claimed themselves "free towns." Sopron is reported to be in the hands of Freedom Fighters and Hegyeshalom is con-trolled by a revolutionary committee.

But there is a grim report that at Magyarovar, only ten miles from the Austrian border, Red soldiers massacred eighty-five peasants, including women and children. The Russians also are reported to have shot entire families in a number of farms and villages.

There is another report that Ukrainian soldiers in the Red Army are refusing to fight against us, and are begin-ning to join in our struggle against the Russians. I see a confirmation of this while walking back to my apartment. A few blocks from us there is a bridge. As I came by, several Freedom Fighters, together with some bystanders, were near one end of it. A Red Army tank was rumbling up, but instead of firing, the driver, a young Ukrainian, stuck his head out and waved. He stopped alongside our boys, jumped down, and walked away. Three of the Freedom Fighters got in and moved off toward firing in the center of the city.

We learn today that since the 24th or 25th Colonel Pal Maleter, a brilliant soldier, has been organizing a general command of the Freedom Fighters—building the new pa-triot army of an independent Hungary. He has established headquarters at the Kilian barracks.

Today, for the first time since the Communists seized control of our country, we heard church bells ring. For us Hungarians the tolling of church bells at noon has a special

Three of the Freedom Fighters got in and moved off toward firing in the center of the city.

Today, for the first time since the Communists seized control of our country, we heard church bells ringing.

meaning. In the 15th century the Hungarians won a great victory over the Turks at Nandorfehervar. The Pope recognized this as a triumph for Christianity, and directed that in memory of it the bells should ring at noon every day. For ten years the bells have been silent. Today at noon the people of Budapest bared their heads and stood reverently in the streets, listening.

Sunday, October 28

The night has been relatively quiet. This morning all the churches and synagogues are filled with crowds of thankful worshipers—more than on any day for a decade. Today even the official radio broadcast a mass.

We feel that we may be winning our Freedom Revolution. This morning's edition of *Szabad Nep,* the official Communist newspaper, declares:

"We must realize that a great national democratic movement has developed in our country. . . . This movement expressed the workers' claim to become genuine masters of the factories. This movement expresses the human claim of the peasantry to be freed from constant uncertainty of existence and unwarranted vexations, and to be able to live their lives as individual or collectivized peasants as they wish. . . .

"It was love of country which gave this people's movement its greatest strength and fervor and rendered it willing to face even death.

"The demand for the equality and independence of the country is as all-embracing as the mother tongue we speak. It is an eternal shame that there were Communists in leading positions who did not understand the language of their own people. . . ."

Over Radio Budapest, Premier Nagy repeats this interpretation, which is so obviously the truth. "The government rejects the view of the formidable popular movement as a counterrevolution . . . it is indisputable that in this movement a great national and democratic movement, *embracing and unifying all our people,* has developed."

Nagy also says that the A.V.H., the hated security police, will be dissolved. He again promises that the Russian troops will withdraw from all of Budapest. Radio Budapest announces that Red Army tanks are leaving the city, but no one has seen any go. And the A.V.H. was in the streets last night searching houses for weapons.

Although many sections of the city remain peaceful today, Red Army tanks are attacking the Kilian barracks, where three thousand Freedom Fighters under Pal Maleter are holding firm. The Russians have also closed the Danube bridges to all traffic. Red tanks and armored cars are stationed at the bridge entrances. Even those persons who are trying to get from one side of the city to the other in order to locate wounded or missing relatives are not allowed to cross. Red tanks are also posted in front of the Parliament Building and A.V.H. Headquarters.

Food is getting scarcer. In one district, Red troops suddenly opened fire on a long line of people, mostly women, at a food store.

We are heartbroken to see so much of our beloved city on fire. But today we watched a fire that we enjoyed. Work-

The Russians have also closed the Danube bridges to all traffic.

Red tanks are also posted in front of the Parliament Building. . . .

ers and students brought propaganda books, pamphlets and leaflets from "Horizon," the Communist publishers and bookstore on Kossuth Lajos Street. They burned them on the street, in front of the building. We all rejoiced to see these vicious, lying words go up in flames.

All through the day we hear good news from the free radio stations throughout the country. Patriots are in control of the greater part of Hungary, especially in the west and south. Everywhere revolutionary workers' councils and local "national committees" are taking charge. In most areas there is little or no fighting, and good order. (Even in Budapest, with all the violence, there has been no looting. Jewels behind smashed shop windows have lain untouched.)

The local national committees are getting in touch with each other, and can now communicate quickly by the radios that they control. Similar demands are being raised in many parts of the country:

Withdrawal of all Red Army troops.

Equality of economic and political relations between Hungary and the Soviet Union.

Dissolution of the A.V.H.

Recognition of the workers' councils as spokesmen for the workers.

Increase of wages and improvement of working conditions.

Freedom to publish non-Communist newspapers and magazines.

New general elections, with several parties.

But today we watched a fire that we enjoyed. Workers and students brought propaganda books, pamphlets and leaflets from "Horizon," the Communist publishers and bookstore on Kossuth Lajos Street.

They burned them on the street, in front of the building.

Radio Free Gyor adds the demand for withdrawal of Hungary from the Warsaw Pact, and for Hungarian military neutrality.

Seven more divisions of the Hungarian Army have joined us in the fight for freedom; by now nearly our entire army is with us. Only the traitors of the A.V.H., on whose hands is the blood of so many thousands of Hungarians, cling to the Russians.

We hear that in a number of places there are friendly relations between the Red Army troops and the local inhabitants. Radio Free Gyor broadcasts: "The Soviet military commander of Gyor has stated: 'We have no intention of interfering in your internal political affairs. I think that the rising of the Hungarian people against the oppressing leaders is justified.' The commanding officer expressed gratitude to all those who yesterday asked about the Soviet garrison's material needs and gave forty liters of milk for the garrison's children without having been asked to do so."

In a broadcast to the Freedom Fighters tonight, Radio Budapest said: "You have won. . . . Your demands will be fulfilled." But at the same moment, Red tanks were shelling two of the Freedom Fighters' strongholds. Radio Free Gyor declares: "'Revolutionary forces should not give up their arms, because no one can believe in Communist promises."

Monday, October 29
We seem to have reached an impasse. Russian tanks remain in control of key points of Budapest, and have sealed off

Russian tanks remain in control of key points of Budapest, and have sealed off all approaches to the city.

all the approaches to the city. At the same time, our Freedom Fighters hold strong positions, and refuse to accept
a cease-fire or lay down their arms until the Reds pull
out.

Fierce fighting rages in a number of districts, and there
are bloody hand-to-hand street battles. Our Freedom Fighters, most of them without any military training, show aston-
ishing skill. In their improvised units, under commanders
of their own choice, they keep strict discipline. There are
no cowards, and a thousand heroes. Our girls brave the
Russian machine gun fire to carry ammunition and food.

Our beloved city is being turned into ruins. The damage
in many districts is worse than at the end of the Second
World War. Whole blocks look as if they had been through
a bombing raid.

We know from the free radios that much of the rest of the
country is under our control, with the fighting stopped in
most places. But there are alarming rumors that the Russians are sending in more tanks from Rumania, and that
Mikoyan is back again in Budapest.

Red Army tanks are again attacking the Freedom Fighters entrenched in Kilian barracks, Zalka Mate barracks, and
the barracks on Bem Square. But we hear that Budapest air-
port is in our hands.

Today the people began rounding up an enemy who is
hated even more bitterly than the Red Army—the agents
of the A.V.H., the traitorous "security police" controlled
by the Russian M.V.D. For ten years the A.V.H., more ferocious even than Hitler's Gestapo, has filled our lives with

Whole blocks look as if they had been through a bombing raid.

terror and brutality, seized our fathers and brothers in the middle of the night, sent our sons in freight cars to Siberia, tortured us in dark cellars, forced us to confess to fantastic crimes, fenced us in slave camps, shot and hanged Hungarians for the crime of loving their country and the truth.

Some of the most notorious A.V.H. agents are caught and shot at once. The others are arrested and put into prison to await trial—much fairer treatment than we ever received at their hands.

I met a friend of mine who tells me that he saw a crowd of patriots capture a well-known A.V.H. officer. They were ready to kill him—and he deserved killing—until someone said: "Let him go. He is a Jew, and if we kill him they will twist the story, and say we did it because of anti-Semitism." So the crowd let him off; he was trembling with cowardice, and ran off as fast as his legs could manage. In Hungary's past there have been occasional examples of anti-Semitism. Only three years ago, at the time of the so-called "doctors' plot" in Moscow, the Hungarian Communists cooked up a local doctors' plot that was just an anti-Semitic action in disguise. But I have heard of no anti-Semitic acts in our Freedom Revolution. In fact, there are hardly any reports of robbery, rape, looting or other major personal crimes.

For the first time in its history, *Szabad Nep,* the Budapest Communist Party newspaper, talks back to Moscow's *Pravda.* It refutes *Pravda's* lying account of our revolution. "The revelling people of Pest and Buda," writes *Szabad Nep,* "want freedom and a life without fear or terror. They

84

want more bread and national independence. Is this what *Pravda* called an adventure?"

The Revolutionary Committee of Hungarian Intellectuals has issued an Appeal that repeats our key demands: settle relations with the U.S.S.R. on the basis of equality; hold a general and secret election in which the people are able to nominate candidates freely; let the workers' councils manage the factories and mines; guarantee the operation of private craftsmen and retailers; abolish the quota system in the factories; free trade unions and peasant organizations; support individual farmers, make collectivization voluntary, and abolish the system of compulsory delivery of farm products; insure freedom of speech, press and assembly; declare October 23, the first day of the Freedom Revolution, a national holiday.

In the afternoon, the Committee of Hungarian artists adds the demand that officials be prevented from interfering in fine arts and that legal measures be adopted to guarantee full freedom to artists, patrons and art societies. Other guarantees, the Committee insists, should include freedom to travel, sell works of art and arrange exhibitions abroad.

We are saddened to hear from Radio Free Miskolc the account of the funeral for the students and Miskolc citizens who were massacred by A.V.H. gangs. But Radio Free Gyor lifts our hearts again with the message: "We have learned that Soviet troops have started to withdraw from the capital. Troops leaving Budapest have already passed through Szekesfehervar. Do not provoke Soviet troops during this move so that armed clashes may be avoided."

Tuesday, October 30

After a lull yesterday, there was bitter fighting last night, with Red Army attacks on barracks and houses, especially in the 9th and 10th districts.

Today fighting against the Russians has nearly stopped, but there is some shooting in the roundup of A.V.H. agents. Freedom Fighters have successfully stormed A.V.H. headquarters in Pest, and also the Communist Party headquarters in Buda. Some A.V.H. agents have disguised themselves in the uniforms of the regular police, who refused from the beginning to use violence against the revolution.

We find that the Russian tanks and armored cars have actually withdrawn from the Buda half of the city. Everyone is at last beginning to believe that the Russians may really leave. Tanks still remain in Pest, however, though an official announcement declares that the Soviet commander has agreed to their withdrawal by tomorrow morning. But we hear rumors that Red troops are still coming into the country, and bringing even heavier weapons.

Life begins to show signs of returning to normal. The strike is still on in part, but Nagy announces that everyone who returns to work today will get paid for the whole past week. Many show up to get their money. The banks are open, and as newly elected chairman of the M.T.I. revolutionary committee, I go to get the money for the staff payroll.

In the afternoon Imre Nagy delivers an address over Radio Budapest. For a week Nagy has been wavering, but what he now says indicates that in the sweep of the Freedom

Revolution he has finally made up his mind to stand with the Hungarian nation. He announces decisions to carry through a number of our most important demands.

The Cabinet has abolished the one-party system under which the Communist Party alone was allowed to function. A new government has been formed, in which Bela Kovacs and Zoltan Tildy of the Independent Smallholders' Party and Ferenc Erdei of the National Peasant Party are key members.

The government has called not only for Red Army withdrawal from Budapest but for the withdrawal of all Russian forces from all of Hungary.

The authority of the local revolutionary and national councils is to be recognized and legalized.

Zoltan Tildy announces the plan to organize the Freedom Fighters as a National Guard. He states that Peter Kos, the traitor who has misrepresented Hungary at the United Nations, has been dismissed. Compulsory crop deliveries are abolished as of today.

Tildy and Erdei call for the rapid rebuilding of the Smallholders' and the Peasant Parties, in preparation for the promised new elections.

After the political speeches, Radio Budapest makes a confession that is no surprise to the people: "For many years the radio has been an instrument of lies. It lied day and night; it lied on all wave lengths. Not even at the hour of our country's rebirth did it cease its campaign of lies." The announcer concluded with enthusiasm: "The struggle which brought national freedom also freed our radio. Those who spoke those lies are no longer among the staff of the Hungarian radio. We who are now at the microphone are new men. We shall tell the truth."

From this point on, Radio Budapest is changing its name to Radio Free Kossuth.

Today there took place another great symbolic act in the struggle toward freedom. Jozsef Cardinal Mindszenty, the Roman Catholic Primate of Hungary, whose torture and trial expressed the aim of the Communists to crush the spirit of religion in the Hungarian people, has been freed at Felsopeteny, where he has been kept under arrest for the past eight years. We learn that one of the three officers who released him was a Jew, and we feel that this fact is another sign of the unity of the entire Hungarian nation. A new "Association of Christian Youth" has also been formed today, and is gathering members.

Radio Free Kossuth broadcasts an ultimatum signed by "all the personnel of the National Air Defense Command." Our Air Force will bomb the remaining Russian tanks unless they leave Budapest within twelve hours.

At the Kilian barracks, much of which are now almost rubble, Russian tanks and artillery are still shelling Maleter's Freedom Fighters. The city is tangled with wreckage, but food shops are open, and the peasants continue to bring more food in from the countryside.

There was still shooting as darkness fell tonight.

Wednesday, October 31
We wake up to find that the Russian troops and armor are

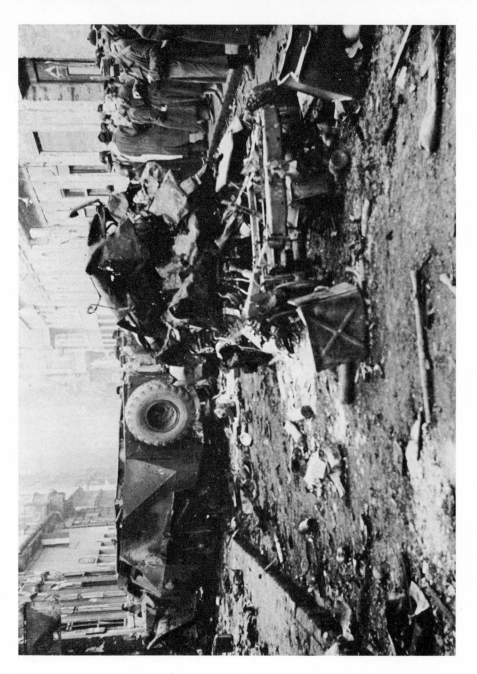

The city is tangled
with wreckage, but
food shops are
open. . . .

completing their withdrawal from Budapest. The final units are at the Parliament Building and the Ministry of Defense. They begin pulling out at 11:00 A.M. By two o'clock in the afternoon they are gone.

Everyone is excited. We stand along the streets and cheer as the Russians leave. No one is working today—everyone is celebrating. Children are playing on the streets again.

We are winning our Freedom Revolution!

The new political parties begin functioning. The Small-holders, Social Democratic, and Peasant Party all bring out newspapers for the first time in many years.

Imre Nagy announces that Hungary plans to withdraw from the Warsaw Pact and to declare its military neutrality.

We are inspired by a broadcast from Radio Free Miskolc: "We shall build up an independent and free Hungary. We shall also create freedom of conscience, a life without fear and a life without slavery. We shall create a life that recognizes only one command: never to forget why Hungary has reached out for arms."

And today I am going to Vienna. As chairman of the M.T.I. revolutionary committee, I am going to carry to the free world my three hundred pictures of Hungary's fight for freedom.

The people of the free world must see for themselves how we Hungarians fought for freedom, how all Hungarians are united, and how great a victory we have won. The United Nations must guarantee a victory, won by such sacrifice and heroism, by protecting a free and secret Hungarian election, in which all the Hungarian political parties can take part. The world must find a way to prevent the Soviet Union from trying again to crush our newly gained liberty. These are the hopes and prayers of the Hungarian people that I will also carry with me.

CHAPTER 3

THE ROAD TO REVOLUTION

Life Under Communism

HUNGARY'S FREEDOM REVOLUTION amazed the whole world because Communist propaganda had sold people everywhere the myth that Russia is invincible and that revolt inside the Communist Empire is impossible. In eight days of October 1956, the Hungarian nation, which has often in the past fought heroically for freedom against foreign oppressors, exploded this paralyzing myth.

This is a mortal blow against the Communist conspiracy to enslave the world. That is why the Kremlin has had to launch a world-wide campaign to try to prop the myth up again. The Communists are desperately afraid that the world—and their own subjects—will not forget that the students and workers of little Hungary defied the whole weight of Russian power, and that the entire Hungarian nation rose up in unity against the Communist tyrants. From the Communist point of view it would be a deadly example for others to follow.

Communist propaganda, made up of lies plus faked pictures, is going full blast in every country. It is trying to make people believe that the Freedom Revolution was the work of "Western agents" or "landlords and capitalists" or "reactionary gangsters" or "gangsters and fascists." The reason for these lies is partly to "justify" the Russian aggression. But the even deeper reason is fear—fear that unless the truth is suppressed, the Hungarian Freedom Revolution will mark the beginning of the end of Communism.

Why did the Hungarian Freedom Revolution break out? How was it that a whole people, an entire nation, fought together against the small handful of fanatical Communists that controlled a foreign-supported regime? How could all the people have shown such courage, such a spirit of sacrifice, such a willingness to face death unafraid rather than bow down any longer? How could young girls and boys, ordinary workers, plain housewives have been so ready to die for freedom? It is not often in history that a whole nation acts in such ways.

I have often been asked such questions as these since reaching the free world. To understand the answers, one must know something about what life has been like in Hungary since the Russian-backed Communists took power ten years ago. The causes of this mass revolt were deep-rooted. They lie in ten years of tyranny, inhumanity, exploitation, hunger, terror and brutality. The breaking point has been reached. The Hungarian nation could no longer passively endure life under Communism. The exact moment when the fighting broke out was partly an accident—due to the shots fired by A.V.H. agents into the backs of the crowd on October 23. But the Freedom Revolution had become inevitable.

The longest, most bitter battles of the Freedom Revolution were fought in the industrial districts, workers' quarters and mining areas. This was natural. The "workers' Paradise" of Communism turned out to be a living Hell. The Communist government has exploited workers more ruthlessly than any other system, slavery included. They have been squeezed tight for the last ounce of energy. No one had better cause than the workers to fight to break the chains that bound them.

The Quota System

In order to increase productivity, every shop and factory has an efficiency expert (*normas*) whose job is to fix the "norm" or quota of work. The quota is the amount an individual worker must turn out in a given time, in order to get his full pay (which is little enough). If he falls short, he is docked.

For example, in a bakery a worker has a quota, let us say, of 20 loaves per hour. One day the efficiency expert shows up. He watches the worker, makes notes, times him with a stop watch, and at the end declares that from now on his quota will be 30 loaves per hour. These experts usually know nothing about baking or any other productive work. They are reliable Communists whose political careers depend on pushing the quotas higher and higher. So it is not hard to imagine how a worker feels to have the support of his family depend on the quota figure set by such a person.

It is typical of the corruption of the Communist regime that these quota experts can usually be bribed. When a worker gives a cut in his wages to the *normas,* the quota gets put at a more reasonable level. This is no guarantee against the expert's coming around the next week to raise the quota again.

Under Communism, the worker is not free to quit his job and look for a better one. If he does he gets in serious trouble. His wages will be reduced, his vacation cancelled, or he may even be sentenced to a period of forced labor.

With this quota system, one result is a foregone conclusion. As the quota is jacked up, the quality of the goods produced gets continually worse.

Stakhanovites

Another trick used in the merciless drive to step up production is the forced competitive system of "Stakhanovism," taken from the Russian example. The professional scabs who spark this system are called "Stakhanovites."

The Communists recruit Stakhanovites from the ranks of the workers by all sorts of promises, and use them to set up practically impossible quotas that all other workers are then required to meet in order to get their full pay. The Stakhanovite champions or pace-setters are given the most favorable conditions of work: the newest machine: two helpers where ordinary workers get one, etc. (The extra helper will be called a "learner.") But in spite of this plush treatment, the Stakhanovites usually over-strain themselves after a while and break down.

The Stakhanovite is one of the new type of "Communist man" who is not supposed to be interested in anything but his work. According to a standard Hungarian joke, he can't even talk to his sweetheart on a beautiful Sunday afternoon about anything except the factory. In reality he is miserable: tired out, and hated by his fellow workers who despise him as a slavedriver and a stooge of the Communists.

The greed of the Communists does not stop at the fierce exploitation of manpower. They also abuse the mechanical means of production. For example, the Russians imposed a new scheme on Hungarian miners that almost wrecked the entire mining industry. It was known as the "hot pick-axe" work plan. This meant that a machine kept operating for months without ever being stopped. The worker in the next shift would have to get to his post ahead of time in order to take over the machine (the "pick-axe") in a "hot state." There was no letup for man or machine. In time one or both reached the breaking point.

"Produce More Today than Yesterday"

As another example of Red exploiting techniques, take the case of Arpad Loy, a Stakhanovite miner who—in his miner's uniform decked out with epaulettes and rows of decorations—looked more like an army general. I once talked to Loy. He told me how the Communists tricked him into starting still another "movement."

"A reporter and a photographer came to interview me about my work," he said. "I casually mentioned that on that day I had exceeded the quota, and thus done better than the day before. We chatted a while, and they left.

"I was amazed to read the article the next day in the paper. It stated that I had started a new movement called, 'Produce More Today than Yesterday.' That evening I was afraid to face my friends for fear of their resentment.

"The following night I was called in to the Party office, congratulated, and immediately warned that the 'movement' I had started would mean even greater obligations on my part. From then on, I would have to live up to my slogan, and turn out every day more than I had the day before."

According to a popular joke, the Communist newspaper, *Szabad Nep* ("Free People") used this technique in the form: "Lie today more than you did yesterday."

"Social Work"

The Communists also invented numerous devices to cheat workers out of their off-time. The Communists figured that if people had no spare time to think it was easier to keep a firm grip on them.

A new meaning was given to the term "social work." It meant that when the factory whistle sounded it was still not the end of the work day. The workers then had to build roads or so-called "cultural centers," without pay. Such "social work" projects provided the manpower to build the People's Stadium and Stalin Square in Budapest, and these were only two of many other such constructions throughout the country.

Recruiting for "social work" was made on a "voluntary basis." This is the way it was handled. A Party representative would visit a factory and announce: "Comrades, I need three volunteers to help build a cultural center." When no one answered, as was usually the case, he would point at random to three victims who would thus become "volunteer social workers." None of them would dare object, because they would immediately be denounced as imperialist agents or reactionaries. That would mean firing, or even a prison sentence.

"Peace-watch"

There was another form of "social work" called "peace-watch." This meant the job of watchman in public buildings on holidays and weekends.

An uncle of mine, who was a merchant before the Communists confiscated his business, got a clerical job in a factory. He complained to me that he had to work every other Sunday, for nothing, because he had been appointed as a "volunteer" for a "peace-watch."

Non-Party workers were mostly chosen for this kind of assignment. The word "peace" is used by the Communists as a cover for compulsory, unpaid labor. A worker refusing a "peace-watch" would be declared against peace and therefore an enemy of the State.

For anyone in the free world, above all in the West, it is impossible to imagine the low standard of living and the misery which is normal for the people in a Communist-controlled country. In Hungary the father, mother and the children are all compelled to work in order to maintain a minimum subsistence level. The low wages paid by the State are even further reduced by taxes. Five Year Plan Loans, and "peace loans."

Factory Lunch Rooms

While the Communist regime drove the Hungarian worker constantly and forced him to raise production, little was done to provide him with even the most basic necessities. At lunchtime he could either eat what he brought from home, or go to the factory lunch room where he could choose one of just two dishes. Workers jokingly called the first the "wooden bench" meal (referring to the hard wood benches in third class railway cars), and the second the "cushioned" meal. Actually, neither meal furnished enough food value. The newspapers published many letters complaining about the food in the factory lunch rooms, but nothing was ever done about it.

"Peace-Loans"

Beginning in 1949 the Communist government has issued the following announcement once a year:

"Subscribe to the peace-loan for the good of the country and yourself."

Once this announcement appears, a tug of war begins between the Communist agents, who push the subscriptions, and the reluctant workers, who do not want to subscribe. Enforced subscriptions usually amount to 5% to 10% of the workers' earnings. Whoever doesn't subscribe, or needs too much persuading, goes on a black list which means that he will eventually lose his job.

As a sop to the subscribers the government runs a yearly lottery. But the lottery is rigged. The winners are decided in advance by the government. The Communist bosses divide the jackpot among themselves—the winners are always sound Comrades occupying high posts in the Party.

Personnel Files

In the factories and offices, the most dreaded authority is the Office of Personnel, which reports to the security police, the A.V.H. The Office of Personnel has a network of informers whose reports are put in the worker's file. The file contains the worker's life history in great detail, especially any information that might indicate an unfriendly attitude toward the regime.

The worker is under observation not only on the job but in his private life also. Each apartment house has its own Party agent who spies on all tenants. His reports find their way to the personnel files. The system makes it easy for personal enemies to file false or spiteful reports.

Until the Freedom Revolution, no one but the most trusted Communists had had access to these personnel files. During the Revolution, however, many of the files came to light.

Here for instance is one on a friend of mine, which I personally examined. It is typically malicious.

L., born 19——.

Father's name, Z.; origin: worker, baker.

Mother's name, Y.; origin: petty bourgeois, clerk.

L.'s characteristics: L. comes from a petty bourgeois family. His father was a merchant, but his shop was nationalized by the State in 1948. While L. attends to his work regularly, from a political standpoint he is entirely unreliable. He went West in 1944, allegedly because he was taken to a concentration camp by the Nazis, and he did not return home until 1947.

According to the deposition of Comrade K., L. regularly lectures his co-workers on the advantages of life in the West. In 1948 he declared that the confiscation of his father's shop was illegal, and for this reason he lost his job. The same year he was arrested for espionage when information was received that he visited the library of the American legation. He was in the hospital for a few months. Finally, in 1949, he applied for a job in our factory. Twice during 1950 he was under disciplinary investigation for stirring up unrest.

L. declared, in the presence of others, that the Five Year Plan is nonsense, and that Comrade Rakosi, "that bald gnome, had invented just another means of torturing the Hungarian people." This was reported to the proper authorities. The Comrades were of the opinion, however, that because L. was indispensable in his job, no action should be taken against him for the time being. The Comrades recommended that we re-educate L. He has ceased to correspond with his relatives abroad.

In 1951 L. married a trusted Comrade, D. Comrade D.

has promised that she will help in the re-education of L. Since then L. has attended the Party meetings, but he is very passive. We frequently send activists to visit him, but when they tried to enlist him as an agitator, he claimed sickness. He always goes to the factory wearing a tie and hat, thus emphasizing his petty bourgeois origin.

At the suggestion of Director S., we sent young Comrade M. to work with L. and to conduct conversations with him. It was agreed that as soon as Comrade M. learned L.'s skills, we would eliminate L. from the factory.

Comrade F. attacked L. at a Party meeting, accusing him of immoral family life and drinking. To which L. gave a cynical answer, saying that when he married D. he didn't know he was getting a Party Secretary instead of a wife. Comrade L. was discharged.

I knew "Comrade L." well. He was an able Hungarian engineer, who during the past few years has had to live on handouts from his friends. His Communist wife left him. While I met him a few months before the Revolution he was penniless, in rags, and hungry. He wanted to escape from Hungary.

I met him again in the first days of the Freedom Revolution. He waved happily to me and said: "Now we don't have to leave our beloved Hungary. We will build a Paradise for ourselves right here at home."

Sickness and Medicine

The ever growing demands for more production, the unbeatable quota system, the Stakhanovite slave-drivers, all contribute to the physical breakdown of the workers, who overflow the hospitals. The tightening ring of the informer network, the constant fear of what a slip of the tongue can lead to, the complete lack of respect for human dignity— these things have driven many people nearly insane. The knowledge that the nation's borders were sealed tight added to feelings of desperation and hopelessness.

What does the government do to help the worker who has collapsed under the Communist system? How do the Communists make good on the slogan that hangs from the wall of every medical consultation room: "To us, man has the greatest value"? Or the slogan that says: "Even foreign medicine cannot cure everything"?

A sick worker must first see the doctor in his own factory, who in most cases is either a Communist or a friend of the factory's Party leaders. The factory doctor is instructed to allow sick benefits only in extreme cases.

For example, B. is sick at home with a fever, and reports to his factory doctor. The doctor sends word to him the next day that since he has a fever he should see the district physician. B.'s condition gets worse. He sends for the district physician, who tells him that he is too busy to visit him, and anyway, with a fever of only 102° F. it is still possible to go out "if the patient is warmly dressed." B. then gets dressed and goes to the doctor's office. After waiting for two or three hours, he is examined, found sick, provided with medicine, and sent home.

But this is not all. B. is now visited by the factory investigators, who check up to see whether he really is sick. After the visit they will write a confidential report about the sick B. and his home, along some such lines as this:

Date, ———. Sick visit to B.'s home. Comrade B. was in bed, and according to his wife had a fever of 102° F. He lives in a petty bourgeois home; he even has a radio and an armchair. Among his books are Stalin's works. However, his bookshelves are mostly filled with decadent Western literature. On the walls there are only family pictures, and our great Communist leaders are not represented. Comrade B. reports that he is very anxious to return to work, as the sick benefit he is getting is inadequate.

Signed, ———

The real purpose of the visit is obvious.

The second slogan—"Even foreign medicine cannot cure everything"—is interesting. Foreign medicine means medicine of Western manufacture, which reaches Hungary in small quantities only. Its distribution is carried out in typically Communist fashion.

For instance, Kutvolgy Road Hospital, where the Communist bosses are looked after, receives this medicine first. If any is left over, it goes to those clinics where Communists of lower grades are treated. The ordinary worker gets nothing from foreign medicine but the slogan on the wall.

Trade Unions

Under the Communist system, trade unions have a special

meaning and role. They are used as enforcement arms of the government. There are so-called steel, textile, food-workers, printers unions, etc., but none of them represent the workers' interests. Trade union membership is compulsory and a worker pays a membership fee that averages over 1% of his monthly wages.

The main function of the trade unions is to organize work-competitions that speed up production. These trade unions meet monthly after work for about three or four hours. The workers realize that it is useless to present any grievances at such meetings. Knowing that workers do not like to attend, the trade union chairmen have to mobilize the Communist party stewards to put on pressure.

It is also the trade unions' task to supervise vacations through the so-called Vacation Secretaries. According to official statistics, about 10 to 12% of the workers are chosen to spend their vacations in State resorts. The other workers can't afford any vacation at all. Judging by my own experience, these State vacations are not to be envied. The time I went on one, the Vacation Secretary dictated our every movement, and all waking hours had to be accounted for. Breakfast at 8:00 sharp, lunch at 1:00, supper at 8:00. If anyone was late, he got nothing to eat. Individual activity apart from the official program was frowned on and not permitted. Sometimes I wanted to read, but they made me dance, or play children's parlor games.

From 1945 to October 1956 there were no strikes in Hungary. Not, of course, because the workers were satisfied. According to the Communist doctrine, everything belongs to the workers, so that if workers strike they strike against themselves. The reasoning is a fraud, but the A.V.H. is strong.

On the other hand, the Communist press eagerly reports in detail any strike that takes place in the outside world.

Unemployment

As the economy became more and more depressed by Communist "planning," the government made desperate moves to avoid complete bankruptcy. *"Economize!"* became the slogan. Official orders and propaganda articles urged factory managers to reorganize their plants to get the same production with less labor. But no plans were made to provide new jobs for the workers fired in this economy drive. The result was widespread unemployment and the miseries that go with it.

Beginning in 1954 tens of thousands of workers were discharged with only two weeks severance pay and no prospects for reemployment. The economy drive hit mostly those who had suspicious entries in their personnel files—and this meant many of the most skilled and efficient workers.

People lived in fear of literal starvation. Many of my countrymen who lost their jobs escaped their miseries by suicide. The Communists, waking up to the seriousness of the situation, tried to calm the people with soothing newspaper articles that promised new jobs for the unemployed. But you can't eat newspapers.

Such were the conditions under which the workers'

hatred grew to a point where only a spark was needed to
ignite it.

According to the Communists, workers and peasants have a
common cause. This is true. The peasants and workers are
bound to the same yoke, and they fear the same terror. However, the atrocities committed by the Reds against the
peasants were even worse than those against workers in the
cities.

When in October 1948 the Rakosi regime began to show
its teeth, it was a generally accepted opinion among the
people that the resistance of the peasants, who would sooner
die than lose their beloved land, would finally break the
back of Communism. Many peasants did die in prisons and
concentration camps, rather than give up their land or com-
promise with the Reds. Among all the peasants the Communists found stubborn antagonism and resistance.

Land Reform

The Reds tried their full bag of tricks to soften up the
Hungarian peasant and bring him closer to Communism.
To begin with, the Communists claimed all credit for the
breakup of the large estates and the distribution of their
land to the peasants. The fact is that right after World
War II, a land reform was carried out by a coalition government. Large land holdings were confiscated and parcelled
out to the peasantry. The peasants did not guess that a few

years later they would have to *give up* most of these lands *to* the Communists.

Week-end Propagandists

Another device used to win over the peasants involved "voluntary week-end propagandists" who visited the villages. These were either Communist agitators or workers pressed into special Sunday "social-work" duty. The idea was to explain and "sell" Communism to the peasants.

These agitators would set out on Sundays in trucks decorated with flags, and swoop down on the villages, where they described the wonders of collective life. No sooner did the peasants realize the true purpose of the visits than they locked their doors. I know personally that in the village of N—— the peasants got together and chased the agitators out with pitchforks. In another village, a peasant received the "people's educator" with courtesy and, once the propaganda line started spouting, cut him short with: "Listen Comrade, if you talk to me about socialism any longer I won't answer for my actions." Whereupon he grabbed a club and made for the propagandist.

Collective Farms

The regime's bureaucrats added their efforts to those of the agitators. Among these were the organizers who pressured the peasants into joining the collective farms (*kolkhoz*). At first they would try peaceful persuasion by describing the advantages of the collective system. If this approach did not succeed, another wave of Communist bureaucrats would come with threats. If all these attempts were unsuccessful, reprisals followed.

The unfortunate peasant who balked was taxed so heavily that it was impossible for him to meet his payments, either in money or produce. The produce collector and the Communist police would harrass him constantly by searching his house from top to bottom. His son would be thrown out of the school because the father was an "enemy of the people." Sometimes the agitators would even enlist the help of the A.V.H. to go to work on stubborn peasants. Rakosi himself publicly acknowledged, in his speech of self-criticism, that there had been many "excesses" in organizing the collectives.

By using these various pressures the collectives slowly started to take form. The establishment of a new collective farm was used as a pretext for Communist festivity. The propaganda machine would be mobilized; press and radio would be on hand to report the great event. At the celebration, the chairman of the collectives would be handed a bouquet of flowers, after which he would tell in a few simple words how happy he was to be freed of his land, his horse, his cow and the rest of his property.

These festivities and radio programs were cordially hated by everyone. The Hungarian sense of humor, always strong even in trouble, gave rise to a joke which was very popular in those times and has spread all through Eastern Europe. It went like this:

An announcer on the Hungarian radio visits a collective

farm and addresses the following words to the peasant who has just joined up:

"Uncle Joe, here is the microphone; say a few words."

The peasant looks skeptically at the mike and says:

"Tell me, where will they hear me?"

"Everywhere in the entire world," is the answer.

"In Europe too?" asks Uncle Joe.

"Yes, of course," says the announcer.

"Will they hear me in America?" says Uncle Joe.

"Sure, they'll hear you there too."

Whereupon Uncle Joe quickly grabs the mike and in a loud voice shouts: "HELP! HELP!"

This is a joke, but it expresses accurately the bitter dissatisfaction of the peasants, and the tragedy of the little man deprived of his few possessions.

Soon after joining the collective farms, the peasant learned that no matter how much he worked, his earnings were no greater than those of others who worked much less than he. Wages were not paid according to individual accomplishment but collectively. It is no wonder that the collective farms became debt-ridden and often bankrupt, and needed constant help from the State just to survive.

Notwithstanding all efforts, the Hungarian countryside before the harvest had a very uneven look. Wherever the grain was high it was the property of one of the remaining individual farmers. Where the grain was poor or stunted it was a collective farm, and this in spite of the fact that the individual farmer worked by himself without machines, while the collective farmers had tractors, combines, harvesting machines, etc. Apart from a few show places like Karcag and Mezotur, the collectives were doomed, in spite of all the government aid. The Hungarian peasant has never forgiven the Communist regime. He has retaliated by withholding what could not be taken by force—his will to work, his know-how and his ingenuity.

Among the problems confronting the regime was that of the "kulaks." In the beginning, only those peasants who employed hired farm hands and who possessed about 100 acres or more of land were considered to be kulaks. Later, the term was used for any peasant whom the Communists disliked.

If a peasant had a nice house to which a Communist functionary took a liking, the peasant would go on the kulak list. Whoever was on that list was a lost man in the People's Democracy. His house would be confiscated and his family deported. His neighbors would be afraid to talk to him, since it was considered a crime to have contacts with a kulak.

If the work on a collective farm was unsatisfactory, a few kulaks were arrested as the most likely culprits. If a village did not furnish enough produce to fill its quota, the authorities would search some kulak farms at night to make up the remainder. The peasants, haunted by the name of kulak, and broken by fear, offered their possessions to the State and went to work in factories or mines to try to escape persecution.

An article written by the Communist Minister of Popular Education, Joseph Darvas, for the Communist newspaper, *Szabad Nep,* shows the mood of the peasantry:

"In May 1953, at the time of the elections, I again visited the country districts. I was told that I would be assigned the most difficult territory, and that's how I happened to go to the Ligetalja district. The previous day I had made an election speech at Nyiregyhaza before ten to fifteen thousand people. This huge crowd stood there silently—no applause, no protests were heard. Its bottomless silence was both dreadful and depressing.

"Later I went to Biri, and there I visited individual homes. In one of these I found a lone woman. She was leaning over a wooden trough and went on washing without answering my greeting. No matter what I asked her there was no reply. She just kept on scrubbing, like someone who wanted to scrub the whole world clean. The black kerchief which covered her head and kept her face in the shadow made her look almost like my mother. She too used to pull her kerchief over her face when angry with me. After a long silence the woman looked up at me with eyes full of anger and went to the cupboard, took out a piece of black bread and threw it in front of me on the table, saying: 'Everything has been taken from us. They have cleaned out the attic. This is all I have left for a whole week. What can I give my family to eat?' "

And this is the same question asked by thousands and thousands of peasants who lost their farms and possesions to the Communist collectives.

It is no wonder that when the Freedom Revolution exploded, the peasants at once joined forces with the students and workers to throw off their oppressors—the Russians and their Hungarian Communist puppets. It is the peasants who kept the fires of the revolution alive with food hauled in from the farms and given free to their fellow Hungarian patriots on the battle line.

HOUSING

The housing shortage was a nagging worry of the Hungarian workers and their families. In Budapest and other large cities, the construction of new houses and apartments did not keep up with the increase of population. In the years just before World War II, quite a few modern apartments had been built in Budapest, replacing many of the old unsanitary tenements. But during the war a large number of buildings were destroyed by the air raids and the German-Soviet street fighting. In January, 1945, Budapest looked like a ghost city. Some experts thought that many years would be needed to rebuild it.

The energy and hard work of the Hungarian people did wonders. From 1945 to 1948—that is, before the Communists took over complete control of the country—the people cleaned out the ruins and started to rebuild. They cleverly remade all usable space, including empty stores and offices, into living quarters.

When the Communists seized total power in 1948, progress along these lines stopped at once, because they were not in the least concerned with the basic needs of the people. Instead, their building program consisted of a showpiece

From 1945 to 1948 —that is, before the Communists took over complete control of the country—the people cleared out the ruins and started to rebuild.

subway, which never got finished, fancy military barracks, and an unfinished sports stadium.

Co-Tenancy

Under the circumstances, the device of co-tenancy became widespread. There was a Communist housing office in every city district, but it did nothing about creating new living quarters. Its job was to regulate co-tenancy.

Just what is co-tenancy? For example: a family of four lives in an apartment that has two bedrooms, a small kitchen and a foyer. The foyer leads into the first bedroom, which in turn has a door into the second bedroom. The second bedroom can also be reached through the bathroom.

One day the housing office assigns this second bedroom to another family, with four children. From then on, life in the apartment is unbearable. In the morning the bathroom is like a station platform. The children get into fights, and the two mothers of course can't get along peacefully in the one small kitchen. Needless to say, there is no family privacy.

Hundreds of thousands of Hungarians have been living like this. Conditions were made still worse by the forced industrialization, which pushed thousands of peasants into the cities to work in factories. Most of them brought their families along. Since the housing offices could not find apartments for them, they all had to jam in as co-tenants.

There was a movie, "Ninotchka," based on a story by the Hungarian writer Menyhert Lengyel, that we saw in Hungary around 1940. I remember the room in Moscow divided by a curtain, in which two entire families were forced to live. The Russian life shown in that movie, which then seemed to me just a witty satire, became a sordid reality in Hungary under Communist rule.

Life in the scarce, very high-rent furnished rooms was even worse than co-tenancy.

The Struggle for Space

Before the war, many people in Budapest lived in good-sized apartments, and some had private houses in the suburbs. These were once fine homes; many of them are still standing, but the residents have changed. The old owners were deported in 1951, or arrested on trumped up charges. The houses were taken over by the Communist bosses. Barbed wire, and A.V.H. guards with watchdogs, now shield them from curious eyes.

While the leading Communists lived in luxury, the dwellings of ordinary workers were not fit for human beings.

Between 1949 and 1951 small shops were gradually eliminated, either through nationalization or direct liquidation or because the government had cut off the supply of goods. The family that could rent one of the stores made empty in this way was lucky, even if it had no running water or facilities for cooking and heating. The new tenant would set up a stove, and pipe the smoke out into the street. Such living quarters were considered wonderful compared to the occupied cellars and wet hovels, in which tuberculosis flourished.

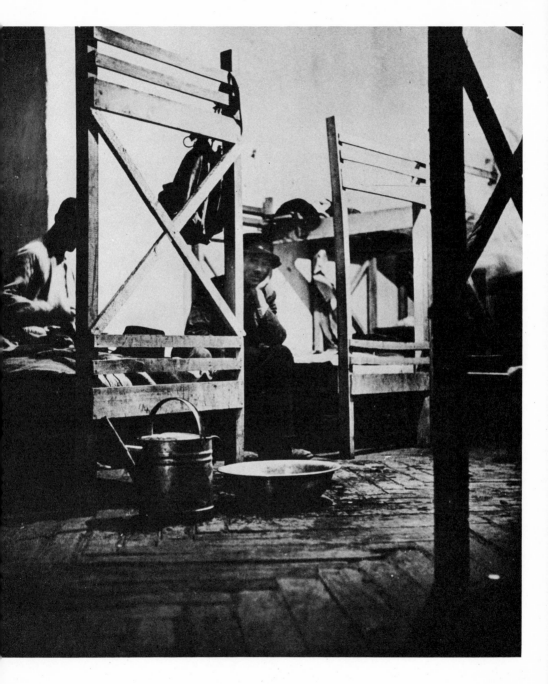

While the leading Communists lived in luxury, the dwellings of ordinary workers were not fit for human beings.

The housing crisis became so acute during the past two years that even the Communist government felt something had to be done about it. The Communists would have liked to send back to the farms some of the peasants whom they had dragged to the cities during 1950/51. But these people, many of them young men and girls, had become used to city living and did not want to return to the villages.

So the government started big housing projects—but only in the columns of the Communist newspapers. In reality, hardly any houses or apartments were built, and the few that they did produce left much to be desired. Not long ago I talked to a Party official who had wangled a new two-room apartment. He said the place was not fit for pigs. Months after he and his family moved in, the walls were dripping with moisture, their clothing got mouldy in the closets, and their food spoiled.

The materials used in building apartments were of poor quality. If the cardboard door was slammed shut by the wind, the plastic doorknob would fall off. But even these low-grade apartments were assigned to Party members only.

The housing shortage was so acute that many young people could not get married simply because they could find no place to live. I knew of a young engineer, V. K., who was promised by his factory manager in 1954 that he would be assigned an apartment. On the strength of the promise, he married his fiancee. Until they could get the apartment, they planned to continue living with their families, who were crowded into co-tenancy quarters. The couple waited patiently for months, but the promise was never kept. The apartment had been turned over to someone with more pull. V. K. got discouraged, quarreled with his boss, and was fired.

He was a skilled engineer, and was able to get another job. But to get an apartment was another matter. Sometime later, he and his wife heard that there was an eighty-six-year-old lady, living as a co-tenant, and very sick. If the young wife took care of the old lady, the couple would get a priority on the co-tenancy room after her death. Seeing no other hope, V. K.'s wife accepted the arrangement—and has been taking care of the old woman ever since. Would she confess even to herself how much she wants her patient to die?

EDUCATION

Communist Seminars

Communist indoctrination was handled through "seminars," held in factories, workshops, schools and universities. All workers and students had to attend, after regular hours. A special Communist school for housewives was organized by the M.S.T. (Communist Women's Society).

Other seminars were conducted in the retail cooperatives where many expropriated merchants and small businessmen worked. They were taught in the seminars how splendid it was that the government had liberated them from their shops and possessions, which were now being held in "socialist safekeeping."

Besides teaching Marxist doctrine, the seminars glorified

Lenin, Stalin, and the Hungarian Communist boss, Matyas Rakosi. At weekly lectures we were tormented with the ideological explanation that all the Communist terror and robbery were carried on for our own good.

Seminar teachers constantly complained that their students were very passive and never asked questions. The truth is that many of us were dead tired and fell asleep. The rest were uninterested or bored.

The seminars were run by Party officials, often women, who were instructed at the main Communist propaganda schools. Their education—if the word can be used at all—was altogether one-sided and covered only official Communist ideology. Stalin's works were treated like Divine Revelation. However, when de-Stalinization set in, his books were sent back to the paper mills. In the seminars, the same teachers who had glorified him now called him a criminal.

In the months just before the Freedom Revolution, many people began to refuse to sign up for the seminars, or to attend if they were already enrolled.

Children and Communism

The main goal of Communist education was to capture the minds of Hungarian youth. Budapest was still in postwar ruins when the government began to build the so-called "pioneer" miniature railroad in order to attract small children. Whenever a foreigner visited town, this railroad was the first "Communist achievement" that they showed him. Needless to say, they didn't call his attention to the fact that even ten years after the war Hungarians still had to travel in freight cars.

Rakosi and Erno Gero often visited the pioneer railroad, to be photographed by the "court photographer," Tibor Bass.

Young children were organized in the "young pioneer" movement, where their Communist education began. In winter they listened to Red propaganda in the schools; in summer they listened to the same thing in the pioneer camps.

The uniforms that the young boys and girls had to wear recall the way Nazism and Fascism handled the youth.

Much of the Communist instruction was directed against religion. Priests were held up to ridicule, and religion in general was put in the most unfavorable light possible. I remember the despair of a friend of mine when his little son, just back from a pioneer camp, asked him: "Daddy, is Comrade Stalin the good Lord?"

Children were introduced to the Communist informer system at an early age. The leaders of the Communist pioneer movement taught their young victims to lie, spy on others, and at all times to be rude and aggressive. These methods were to be used with their own families. The Communists made strong efforts to break down parental authority, which in Hungary has always been strong. Unfortunately, some of the children fell for this teaching, and not only spied on their parents but rebelled against them.

A teacher's job was not easy. Much of the schoolroom space had been taken over for other purposes. In the cities,

The uniforms that the young boys and girls had to wear recall the way Nazism and Fascism handled the youth.

many classrooms were used for Communist meetings, and for training propagandists to send into the villages. In the country, a large section of the school building, sometimes the whole building, would often be used as a barn to house animals or store grain belonging to collective farms. All this made for an acute shortage of schoolroom space.

Drugs in the Classroom

The Communists are guilty of having brought into the schools one of the most injurious practices known to mankind: the use of drugs.

A neighbor of mine told me that her child (a little girl) came home from school one day in a sort of daze. Upset by her unusual behavior, she immediately took her to a doctor, who was unable to find out what caused her condition. My neighbor then took the child back to the school. The teacher admitted bluntly: "Your child was unruly, so I gave her some 'sevenaletta' with her lunch to quiet her down. I often give this drug to jumpy children who don't sit quietly as they should, with their hands behind their backs."

This practice became such a scandal that even *The Literary Gazette,* one of the leading official magazines, protested against it.

History Rewritten

Elementary as well as high school textbooks were changed so as to fit in with Communist doctrine. To suit "dialectical materialism," the Communists rewrote not only historical texts but even the books on physical science. Hungarians laughed off as jokes the ridiculous Russian claims that the Russian, Popov, invented radio, and that the incandescent lamp was invented by some obscure Russian scientist.

The Russians even forged letters proving that Isaac Newton recognized the superiority of Russian physicists. The science of jet propulsion was claimed as the brainwork of another unknown Russian genius.

These lies were fed to the children in the schools, and it was only with great effort that the parents could set them straight at home.

High school students were required to put in many extra hours studying Marxist ideology and the Russian language.

The Communists were trying by every possible means to dominate the Hungarian youth completely. But their seeds fell on barren soil, and they harvested scorn and contempt. The Hungarian young people were clever enough to learn quickly how to see through the whole business, and to put on a pretended air of enthusiasm and cooperation.

The Universities

Only selected high school graduates could go on to the universities. The questionable privilege was reserved for two types. The first were the children of 100% loyal Communist Party members. These were the pampered little Bolshevik-aristocrats, who were taken to and from school in bullet-proof limousines, to protect them from contact with the offspring of "common" people. The second group that went on to universities was limited to children of "pure" worker or peasant stock. If a student's father happened to have been a former small tradesman, the student was registered as "capitalist origin" and blocked, as a general rule, from higher education.

The unchallenged master of the university was not the Rector, Chancellor or Dean, but the leader of "the study group," who usually had no more than an elementary and Party school training. These poorly educated Party hacks, forced on the universities by the government, decided on the program of studies. They were also charged by the Party with getting rid of the professors who were judged unreliable from a Communist standpoint.

Assigned as special teachers were a host of other Party functionaries who as time went on got more and more power. Their job was to teach Marxism, military science, and the Russian language. These Red professors were trained for their jobs in Communist seminars, where they were taught the basic elements of Marxism, the glorification of such Communist heroes as Stalin and Rakosi, and public speaking. The more promising were sent through advanced seminars where they received a more thorough grounding in Communist ideology. With their limited intellectual baggage, they were felt to be reliable, since they could only parrot what they had learned by rote. This, and nothing more, is exactly what the Party expected of them.

Once his university studies were completed, a graduate had no guarantee that he would find a decent job. The best jobs were given to Communists, and only those posts for which there were no Communist candidates—as might be the case as in a highly specialized field of knowledge—went to the non-Communist graduates.

Blind Alley

Only Hungarian students found reliable by Communist standards were permitted, then, to get a higher education. This meant the children of trusted Party members, factory workers, and the poorest peasants—in other words, those who, under the Communist regime, would seem to have had the most to gain by the Red system. Perhaps the best proof of the failure of Communism is provided by these "reliable" young men and women.

Despite the preferred treatment given them by the regime, they turned on their master, and joined—often led—the Freedom Revolution. Why was this so? It was because they, like all the nation, were aware that Communism was leading them into a blind alley.

Hungarian youth reached a point where the Red promises of a golden future no longer held any meaning. The Communists had falsified and rewritten Hungarian history, but the students still managed to learn how their ancestors had fought off foreign oppressors in the past. The examples were brought up to date.

FAMILY

In Hungary the Communist regime has always tried to destroy traditional family life. Any non-Communist social unit, however small, is a possible pocket of resistance to Red domination.

Hungarian youth reached a point where the Red promises of a golden future no longer held any meaning.

The Communists undermined the family by forcing women and children to work, by crowded living quarters and by other special devices that they invented.

The economy is so organized that a Hungarian husband and his wife very often have quite different working hours, and may not see each other for a week at a time. This forced separation plus the added annoyances of co-tenancy cause misunderstandings in the home and often lead to divorce.

Between 1949 and 1954 the government made big efforts to increase the population, in order to have more recruits for the labor system. The Communists encouraged people to have children, even out of wedlock. In the latter case, the babies were placed in government nurseries, and the mothers went back to work.

Because they wanted a population increase, the Reds prohibited abortions. Doctors who performed abortions were given severe prison sentences. Before long the government nurseries were filled with babies.

By 1954 the birthrate had nearly doubled, but no new nurseries had been built, nor were there enough schoolrooms and teachers to handle the education of the expanding numbers of children.

When the Hungarian regime could no longer deal with the situation, they appealed to Moscow and were given permission to "stop" births. Abortions were thereupon permitted; and were, in fact, performed free of charge in the government hospitals.

Following the Russian pattern, the Hungarian Communists used every means to turn the children against their

The Communists undermined the family by forcing women and children to work. . . .

parents. We were told that in the Soviet Union a public statue had been put up to a son who had denounced his father to the police. This was the example Hungarian youth was to follow.

Hungarians have a deep sense of religion and strong family traditions. In spite of all the effort of the regime and in spite of the drab, hopeless everyday existence, the family survived. But the constant struggle to preserve the family from the relentless attacks made our personal lives a torment.

RELIGION

The Last Rampart

Once the Communist regime had cut the Hungarian nation off from the outside world, the people had only one consolation left—their faith in God. People who had in the past hardly ever gone to Mass, listened to a sermon or attended synagogue now went regularly to religious services. But the Reds were not long in reacting.

The Communists arrested the head of the Catholic Church in Hungary, Cardinal Mindszenty, who was the major spiritual symbol of resistance to Communism and its atheistic doctrine. The Cardinal, trusted by all, represented the last barrier. He paid bitterly for his courage. After imprisonment and torture, he was given a mock trial, and sentenced on charges that everyone knew to be false.

Then the Communist drive against all Catholic, Protes-

The Cardinal, trusted by all, represented the last barrier. He paid bitterly for his courage.

tant and Jewish church leaders, and all religion, began in earnest.

Persecution

Clergymen of all faiths were arrested without cause, or transferred to remote parts of the country. The regime did not dare to close the churches and synagogues, but the worshipers who went to them came under immediate suspicion. Religion and the clergy were made the targets for abuse and ridicule by the Communist agents and propagandists. As a prime example, a Catholic church was torn down to make way for the huge, hideous metal statue of Stalin.

Before the Communists came, all children customarily were given instruction in the schools in their religions. The Communists soon put an end to this. They prohibited the teaching of religion in the schools. They "permitted" private religious instruction, but strongly "recommended" against it. Homes known to be religious were visited and threatened by Party agents.

In spite of these repressive acts, the people kept on going to the churches and synagogues. When they did not dare to go, they prayed all the more at home. One Chairman of a cooperative whom I knew had a life-sized bust of Stalin in his office. His wife and mother-in-law had made a religious shrine in their home, before which they all prayed. The Communists could not smash the spiritual life of the nation. The people clung to religion as their last hope and last comfort, that gave them spiritual protection against the Communist terror.

. . . a Catholic church was torn down to make way for the huge, hideous metal statue of Stalin.

A striking example of Communist cynicism is the way they exploited the Hungarian love of sports. The government set up a Committee on National Physical Training and Sports (O.T.S.B.) under the direction of Gyula Hegyi, an old friend of Party boss Matyas Rakosi. This Committee was responsible for the top Hungarian athletes, and it gave them good paying jobs. These jobs were, of course, a formality to preserve their amateur status in international competition.

Pawns of the State

Under the Communist system, all athletes are really professionals, even though all profits from sporting events go to the government. The best athletes spend most of the year in training camps, away from their families. Not long ago I talked to one of them who was complaining that he hardly ever had a chance to see his wife and child. He admitted that he had an easy life in the Tata training camp, but he knew that as soon as he stopped producing victories for the government he would be dropped. Since he had no industrial or professional training, he lived in fear of a poverty-stricken old age.

It was well known that leading athletes who went abroad to compete came home with a lot of things not to be found in Hungary. In the beginning they were careful to include only presents for their families. Later they began to smuggle on a large scale. In one case the players on Hungary's World Champion Soccer team smuggled in several thousand pairs of nylon stockings. The O.T.S.B. punished several players, among them Gyula Gusics, the outstanding goal-keeper, by suspending them for a year. To avoid unpleasant publicity, however, this affair was not taken to the courts. The government must have been well aware of the practice all along, but it did not interfere for a long time, and then only when the smuggling got out of hand.

The teams were always accompanied on their foreign trips by one or more Comrades who were trained political agents. Despite this precaution, some of the athletes sought and found political asylum in the free world. While news of such matters never appeared in the Communist newspapers or over their radio, we managed to learn about it. There was much speculation and discussion among the people on this whole subject.

Sugar Coating

Sporting events were shrewdly used by the Communist regime to turn the attention of the Hungarian people away from their dreary everyday existence. In Budapest a large and beautiful stadium was constructed, which turned out to be a profitable investment for the government, even in a financial sense. At a good soccer game there would be 100,000 paid spectators.

The Communists believed that by winning victories abroad Hungary's athletic teams would prove the superiority of Communism. They therefore thought that such victories were very useful propaganda tools, and were convinced that "bourgeois elements" in foreign nations were much impressed by them. Moreover, the teams touring abroad, especially the world-famous soccer team, also brought back a lot of foreign exchange credits. But though Hungary needed these credits badly, the Russians took most of them for their own purposes.

Soccer is the most popular sport in Hungary. During the time of the world championship soccer tournament in Switzerland, in 1954, everyone listened to the radio broadcasts of the games. The Hungarian team had bad luck, and lost. In their bitterness at losing a victory that the soccer fans had thought certain, they blamed Gustav Sebes, vice-president of O.T.S.B. The fans staged a demonstration that night, and threw stones through the window of Sebes' apartment. A large crowd also gathered in protest before the building of *Szabad Nep*, the Party newspaper. The Russian bosses of the A.V.H. appeared quickly at the scene and scattered the crowd. In looking back on this tense and emotional scene, I have often thought that conditions then were already so bad in Hungary that only a spark would have been needed to transform a soccer fan's rather foolish protest into a revolution.

Bets on sporting events were another source of income for the State. The public as a whole lost plenty on gambling. Thirty per cent of the total wagered was divided among the winners, and the government pocketed the remaining 70%.

During the spring of 1956 articles appeared in the Communist press reporting that Hungary could send only a small team to the Olympic Games in Australia because the government had no funds. This made everybody indignant, because it was common knowledge that the government had taken in huge sums of money from the big sports events and its 70% take on the government-run betting system.

The Communists then tried to start collecting an Olympic Games fund from the public, but they soon gave that up in the face of the popular indignation. The solution the government finally found was to jack up still higher the government's percentage on betting, calling this a special Olympics contribution.

Under Communism, sports are much more than recreation for the people. They are money-raisers and propaganda weapons for the regime. Athletes have no choice but to work for the State and produce victories for Communism.

POLICE

Under Communist rule, every aspect of life in Hungary is brutally controlled by a special police system. In this respect Communism is the same as Nazism, only more complete. My people have suffered under both. We learned how the Nazis used terror and brutality to enslave us, and we learned the same thing under the Communists. The Nazis "declassed" us on the basis of national, racial and religious origin. The Communists have gone a step further, and put the "untouchable" mark also on anyone with a "bourgeois" background—that is, anyone whose family ever contained property owners, businessmen, intellectuals of ability and integrity, or just anyone with firm patriotic convictions.

Having had full experience with the Nazi Gestapo, my

people know that the A.V.H., the tool used by the Russians to beat down the Hungarians, acts also as a conspiratorial secret police. The A.V.H., like the Gestapo and its Russian model, the M.V.D., has recruited its agents from the most vicious elements in society. The A.V.H. rules by terror, open and concealed. It has no respect for human dignity, religion, or any of the basic rights possessed by citizens of free countries. It is the whip used by the Communists to lash us into submission.

I have indicated how completely this police system ruled our lives, whether in factory, farm, home or church. The Communist bosses make the rules, and the A.V.H. sees that they are obeyed. Those who resist are eliminated.

According to Communist reasoning it is better to sacrifice the lives of one hundred innocents than to let one "enemy of the people" escape. In Hungary, the Communist police state enforced this theory without mercy. During the past eight years, the A.V.H. has murdered tens of thousands of innocent Hungarians, pressed countless others into forced labor and deported thousands upon thousands to internment camps. In May and June 1951 alone, over 60,000 of my compatriots, whom the Communists declared to be "bourgeois elements," were snatched from their homes and exiled to border areas where they either starved to death or committed suicide out of desperation.

Because Nazism was built on hatred, brutality and force, it was doomed to a violent end. The police state of Communism is built upon the same foundations and it, too, must expect the same fate.

In Hungary the Communists used radio, press, films and the theater to flood the country with lies and slogans. But because it was built on lies, the Red propaganda machinery inevitably failed in the long run.

Hungarian-Soviet Society

To begin with, the country's best artists and writers were forced to sell Russian Communism to the people under the label of culture. Various organizations were formed for this purpose. The most important was the M.S.T. (Magyar-Szovjet Tarsasag, that is, "Hungarian-Soviet Society").

M.S.T. entertained lavishly with buffet suppers, which naturally attracted many underfed people. It arranged concerts in which Tchaikovsky was made out to be a Communist agitator, and Moussorgsky a musician who was fighting for the proletariat when he composed *Boris Godunov.*

It was not only famous Russian composers and artists who were thus converted into Communists. By some miracle, a lost letter of Beethoven's would be discovered proving that he was sympathetic to Communist ideology.

At first these concerts were open to the general public, but after a while only paid-up members of M.S.T. would be admitted. The organization rapidly lost members. The concerts and buffet suppers came less often, and were replaced by long, illustrated lectures on "the Soviet Union, the land of victorious socialism." M.S.T. had its own newspaper, the *Uj Vilag* ("New World"), which served as another propaganda tool.

Branches of M.S.T. were set up all over the country. Even factories had branches, with activists whose job was to "invite" the workers to the Society's lectures. Woe unto those who did not attend! Once a year, M.S.T. organized a "Soviet-Hungarian Month," which was popularly referred to as the "Month of the Great Mistake."

Russian "Superiority"

One of the greatest mistakes the Russians made in Hungary was to look down on the Hungarians and to scorn their culture as inferior to their own. This attitude succeeded only in wounding our national pride. The Russians, with their contemptuous feeling of superiority, sent to Hungary only their worn-out films, their oldest dancers, and poorest singers. But they piled on the sauce.

The old films, for instance, fitted out with a new Hungarian sound track, were shown in the largest theaters with a lot of fanfare and publicity. The old dancers, however, could not be made any younger, not even with the best makeup. Under the circumstances, the performances given by these doddering visitors proved to be a complete flop. No matter how much they were advertised, the Hungarian public—well informed in art and music—hooted them off the stage without mercy.

The Russians soon learned that the "Month of the Great Mistake" did more damage than good, so they began sending some of their better artists. It is typical of the fairness of the Hungarian public that Ulanova, a first-rate ballerina, was received with enthusiasm as an artist, even though she was one of the hated Russians.

A typical Soviet-Hungarian Friendship Month would cost a small fortune, with us Hungarians footing the bill.

The Curtain Begins to Fall

The regime gradually sealed off all contacts with the free world. Foreign newspapers and magazines slowly disappeared from the stands. In 1948 it was possible to buy *Illustrated London News, Picture Post* and even some issues of *Life,* but after a while only foreign Communist publications such as the *Daily Worker, L'Humanité* and *Vie Nuove* were available.

Films and illustrated lectures offered by the free world legations drew only small audiences. Most Hungarians avoided them out of fear of reprisal. One never knew whether A.V.H. agents might be posted at the exits to make arrests. The popular library of the American Legation was closed.

We Hungarians were so starved for information about the outside world that we would stand for hours looking at picture displays in the windows of the Information Services of the Western countries. But this too was dangerous, for the A.V.H. often arrested the spectators. Some of us corresponded with relatives and friends in foreign countries, but this also risked investigation by the secret police. For years, theaters presenting Russian movies were empty, while those showing movies made in Western nations had

141

long waiting lines. This proved to be so embarrassing to the government that it prohibited Western movies.

The Curtain Drops

With the planting of mine fields and the erection of machine gun towers, arc lights and automatic flare trippers at the border, the Iron Curtain was lowered in the physical as well as the spiritual sense. Expensive radio-jamming stations cut off news broadcasts and other programs from the free world. Some of these jamming stations, now used by the Communists, had been built by the Nazis. It became dangerous for anyone to listen to broadcasts from the free world.

Music as Enemy

The Communists tended to ban any non-Russian import, including jazz, which they branded as American propaganda and decadent meowing. An article in the magazine *Magyar Radio* ("Hungarian Radio") spoke of the saxophone as a weapon in the hands of the imperialists, and jazz drummers as traitors to the people. It was really depressing to tune in to musical programs, and always to have to listen to Russian songs like "Katyusha" and "Dunyushka." But we got around this by playing and dancing at home to modern dance records. That is, unless a high Communist official lived next door.

Where one did, there was still a way around it. I was once invited to a birthday party where we danced with earphones attached by a long wire to a record player. "A party functionary lives next door," our host explained, "and I

With the planting of mine fields and the erection of machine gun towers, arc lights and automatic flare trippers at the border, the Iron Curtain was lowered in the physical as well as the spiritual sense.

don't dare play my dance records out loud." Youngsters
used to dance a fox trot or boogie-woogie to the melody of
Russian folk songs or Hungarian *csardas*.

As for the press, non-Communist papers like the *Kis
Ujsag* and *Szabad Szo* couldn't get newsprint, and their
editors were arrested. Gradually only the *Szabad Nep* and
a few other Communist-controlled papers, like the *Magyar
Nemzet*, were left.

Russian Wonder-Films

Finally the Communists let loose a flood of propaganda that
they hoped would sweep away all possible forms of resistance. From this point on, the only movies to be seen were
those made in Soviet Russia or in one of the captive countries. But these "wonder-films" were flops. They were
sugary nonsense about the marvels of Communism and the
superiority of "the Soviet man." We watched these movies
with indifference and scorn, especially when, as often, they
falsified historical events of which we Hungarians had been
eye witnesses.

For instance, Russian war movies always showed events in
such a way as to give the impression that it was the Russians
who saved the Western Allies. But all Hungarians knew
that in reality it was only the tremendous flow of Western
help and supplies that rescued the Russians.

It is a matter of record that when the Russians "liberated"
Hungary from the Nazis, they plunged into the most bestial
mass raping of Hungarian women, and looted the country
without mercy. Yet the Russian films and illustrated articles

brazenly pictured the Hungarians as receiving the Russian troops with open arms.

It was during this same "liberation" that Russian soldiers picked both men and women up in the streets to send to forced labor gangs. Hungarians will never forget that many of those who were taken away for *a kicsi robot* ("a little work") came back from the Soviet Union years later, broken in body and spirit.

Inventing News

Every day the newspapers printed articles that were simply invented by the propagandists without any relation to facts. One time I was staying with a peasant family in the small village of Omassa. The first evening I asked my hosts for some light to read by. The old peasant mother walked away without a word, and came back soon with a copy of *Szabad Nep*.

"Here it is," she said. "Here's your light. It says that electricity was installed in our village yesterday. See if you can read by it."

I remember another experience that shows how feature stories were invented in order to falsify conditions. I was ordered to do a photo story on a typical peasant wedding. It was to be a documentary showing pleasant, optimistic peasants in a "happy state of mind." My assistant and I traveled to the village of Derecske. Everything was supposed to have been arranged by the village schoolteacher, who was to find us a place to work in, provide models, and prepare an "atmosphere of optimism."

Apparently something had gone wrong with the atmosphere, because the peasants received us rather gloomily. In order to take the first picture we went to a collective farm meeting room. Waiting for us, we found six peasants who were a horrible sight—unshaven, hair uncut, wearing rags. Bearing in mind that we had to furnish an "optimistic" story, we got hold of the village barber, and told him to give them a shave at the newspaper's expense. Then we went off to take the outdoor pictures.

When we returned to the room an hour later, we found only the barber. There he stood in the midst of a pile of hair cuttings, with soap on his clothes, very anxious to collect his bill, which amounted to about 100 florints.

My assistant asked him, "Does a shave cost that much around here?" "No," the barber replied, "but they told me that they ought to have haircuts too, since the newspaper was paying." "But where are they all?" I asked him. "Oh, they went off to milk the cows that are just back from pasture."

There was nothing to do except wait until the milking was finished. That evening the "wedding" was to take place in the local House of Culture. From the property room of the National Theater we had brought along some artificial fried chicken, sweets, and colored water to serve as wine. But we found it hard to work up much gaiety in our peasants with only fake food and tinted water on the table.

This is the true story behind the smiling peasant faces that appeared in our documentary published in a 1953 issue of the propaganda paper, *Hungary*. And this is how most re-

But we still shouted: "Long live Rakosi! Long live the Party!" Otherwise our neighbor might denounce us to the A.V.H.

ports and documentaries were manufactured by the Communist regime.

The Lie Factory

The chief lie factory was the official Communist newspaper, *Szabad Nep*. Its first editor was the much feared Oscar Betlen. His favorite question to a writer submitting an article was: "What profit does the government get out of this?"

If anyone dared to criticize any aspect of the government's activities, he would be fired. "There is no indispensable man," was the slogan, and only those stayed who could continue to lie without letup. The language of the press became incredibly meaningless and repulsive. We would be sickened by *Szabad Nep's* captions: "Honest men will now gain new hope and strength from the words of the beloved Stalin," or "These are the words of our dear Stalin." Most of us were ashamed of ourselves, and hated ourselves for our cowardice. But still we shouted: "Long live Rakosi! Long live the Party!" Otherwise our neighbor might denounce us to the A.V.H.

The libraries and bookstores were strictly censored. Besides "innocent" classics, there were only books by Communist and "progressive" authors. For anyone who wanted to be in good standing with the regime, it was obligatory to read Russian Communist best-sellers. Among these were the novels written by Alexander Fadeyev, who was hailed as the greatest writer on Communist youth. This was the same Fadeyev who was driven by the Russians to acute alcoholism, and who died in an asylum—probably by suicide—in 1956.

Still, people got so bored with the Party-controlled literature, which did nothing but falsify real life, that they secretly lent each other the works of genuine Hungarian and foreign writers. Alongside the government and factory or office libraries, the system of illegal private libraries built up a big circulation.

Writing for the Party

The quality of Hungarian literature declined rapidly under Communism. Poems, books, plays, articles could not deal with life as it really is, but had to give a picture approved by the Party. The Communists spoke about the need for "socialist realism." This meant, more or less, that the writer was supposed to show a single individual as a type representing the life and way of thinking of the working class or the peasantry. But the writers were not allowed to tell the truth about how the workers and peasants really lived and thought. As a result, what they wrote was empty and dull, and no one was interested in reading it.

Some young writers were good Communists and tried to write according to the Party rules. But somehow even they could not find the right "tone" to make their work convincing. Most of the talented writers were forced to write against their own beliefs, and one could feel this in reading them.

Some writers sold out to the regime. For their treachery, they were allowed to live well. Like the big Party leaders, they were isolated from the people. They wrote about workers and peasants exactly according to the Party line, from the well-furnished rooms of a comfortable home. They didn't care what was really happening among the people, and some of them may not even have known about the actual conditions. One of these official writers was the editor of *Irodalmi Ujsag* ("Literary Gazette"). To show his modesty he wouldn't buy a car, though he had plenty of money. Instead he always used taxis. He had never been on a trolley-bus until one night, when he arrived back from a trip to Moscow, there wasn't any taxi to be found. After that he wrote articles on the marvels of our Communist bus system, and he praised the buses to the skies at every gathering. But he continued, without further exception, to use taxis.

Able writers—often those who spoke several foreign languages—were suddenly arrested in their homes, places of work, or even the street, and imprisoned without any hearing. Their families would not be notified, and could only guess what had happened when the police came to search the apartment, or cancel the lease. In most cases even the police didn't know the reason behind the order, which came from higher up.

Many writers spent years in various prisons, without ever getting a hearing or receiving a court sentence. They were never told why they had been jailed. Years later they might be suddenly released without explanation. Sometimes on release they would be "rehabilitated," and given money and a new apartment. But even after years in prison many of the writers refused to jump on the Party bandwagon.

The government was so hard up for talent and training that sometimes it had to appeal to the writers in prison for help, and to get them to make translations of Party speeches and documents.

It tried to suppress other writers altogether, by forcing them to do heavy physical work. But it is not so easy to bottle up true talent. One of our poets, well known abroad, spent his prison years in the Recsk coal mine. Yet even in the midst of his mine work, he continued to think and create. He was not allowed any paper, so he memorized his new poetry. He completed what amounted to a volume, and then got his fellow prisoners to memorize the individual poems. In this way his poems were published.

The Opera

The only place where one could find a somewhat lower propaganda pressure was at the State Opera. The Communists did not dare to sneak Russian folk music into Rossini's musical scores. But the librettos didn't do so well. Lieut. Pinkerton in *Madame Butterfly,* needless to say, was made out to be a vicious tool of American imperialism who ruined the honor of the simple daughter of the people, Cho-Cho-San. But since the melody stayed the same, the audience paid no attention to the altered librettos, and filled the Opera House to capacity every night.

The zeal of the Communist agitators was gradually stepped up. With true Communist aggressiveness they kept hammering home to us Hungarians the tasks we would have to perform.

A joke, popular in Budapest during one of the regular propaganda drives, describes the visit of an agitator to Comrade Kovacs. The agitator gives his canned talk about how wonderful life under Communism is, and praises the new industrial centers like Stalinvaros. Comrade Kovacs' only comment is: "And am I going to get all this and my winter coat too?"

The Big Promise

The Reds were great hands at promising all sorts of things that they couldn't deliver. When we have built this or that, they would say, everything will be rosy. Five years would go by, and everything would be just the same. The failure of the first Five year Plan was too obvious to hide or deny. But the Communists at once started a second Five Year Plan that was equally doomed to failure from the start.

Budapest, the capital city, was deteriorating. The country was in economic chaos. The population, driven by overwork and persecution, looked into the hopeless future with sunken eyes. The Communists were desperate with their colossal failures and their own uncertainty. Communist propaganda moved into a final phase, which was a confession of defeat.

The "Safety Valve"

Increasing corruption and lawless terror hastened the developing crisis. The "opening the safety valve" operation

—so named by Tibor Dery, a leading writer—began the exposure of many past Communist atrocities and lies. This led to open criticism, first in speeches and then even in the Communist newspapers. Petofi Circle, in Budapest, became the center for such speeches and criticism.

In the beginning, many thought that this would turn out to be another trick, since it was typical of the Communists to use a device of this sort to expose a new batch of "enemies."

The safety valve operation, however, quickly began to get out of hand. Matyas Rakosi, as one of his last desperate acts before being thrown out of power, prohibited all meetings at Petofi Circle. But the valve had opened too far.

It is not generally known that Rakosi, just before he escaped to Russia, drew up a list of 400 people who were to be liquidated. Many of the regular Petofi Circle group were among them.

Backfire

The regime soon realized that it was too late to return to the old ways. It was forced to publish new newspapers, and to give in to more and more demands. The *Hetfoi Hirlap* ("Monday News") appeared on the streets. The public was so eager to buy it that the regular news dealers couldn't keep order and it had to be sold by policemen. This was the first more or less freely edited paper to appear in Communist-occupied Hungary.

The *Irodalmi Ujsag* ("Literary Gazette") began to make changes, and *Muvelt Nep* ("Cultured People") published a few provocative articles. Even *Szabad Nep* went along. There was no stopping the flood. The Communists had exposed themselves in their true colors. Red propaganda had backfired.

Weird Ritual

On October 6, 1956 the regime staged a grotesque funeral, for propaganda purposes, at Kerepesi cemetery. Five years earlier, Laszlo Rajk and his associates had been arrested, tortured and killed by their Comrades for alleged crimes of Titoism, spying for Western powers, and so on. Then in 1956, under the de-Stalinization policy, they were "rehabilitated," and it was officially declared that their earlier trials had been frame-ups.

Now, on October 6, the bodies of Rajk and a number of the others were exhumed, placed on huge biers, and given a public burial. Their murderers gave the funeral orations.

Thousands upon thousands of people went to this incredible ceremony—not because they were forced to and not in organized groups, but by their own choice. We were curious to see for ourselves an event of a kind the world has never before witnessed. We gathered quietly in a strange silence, but our faces reflected the deep contempt and disgust that we felt listening to Apro Antals and other Communist murderers deliver their self-debasing orations.

The monotonous rhythm of the funeral march served as background music to the funeral of Red propaganda. No movie director could have arranged a more fantastic spectacle. Black flags flew wildly in a strong wind. There were dark and threatening clouds gathered in the sky. A violent storm was in the making, and it did not take long for the storm to break out. The Rajk funeral was a warning and an omen.

The last agonizing moments of Communist propaganda came during the historic week after October 23. The editions of the Communist newspapers were burned as soon as they reached the streets. We revolutionaries now published our own newspaper, *Igazsag* ("Truth"). The *Szabad Nep* building, built with money stolen from the people, was demolished. Red propaganda material was drowned in the surge of freedom.

On October 31, Radio Budapest, in the announcement that marked its transfer to the revolution as Radio Free Kossuth, summed up the decade of Communist propaganda in the words that I have already quoted: "For many years the radio has been an instrument of lies. It lied day and night; it lied on all wave lengths."

The goal of the Hungarian Freedom Revolution is to destroy those lies and to put truth in their place.

CHAPTER 4

VICTORY POSTPONED

FOR FOUR DAYS—from October 31 to November 3, 1956— Hungary was free. Although the Russian forces were still in our country, they had withdrawn from the cities and the fighting had stopped. The whole nation recognized the Imre Nagy government, which, knowing it had no other alternative, was ready to carry out the will of the people.

To bring the government still closer to the popular will, it was reorganized once more on November 3. Imre Nagy remained as Premier, along with two other Communists. There were three representatives of the Independent Small-holders' Party, three Social Democrats, two from the Peasant Party and one Independent. The nation was casting off the one-party Communist dictatorship. All of these cabinet members, including the three Communists, had spent years in jail on Moscow's orders.

Four Days of Freedom

And the Hungarian people, in those four days, showed clearly what they wanted. In spite of the Russian tanks in the background, everyone spoke without fear in those four days of freedom. No one was censored.

In his address of November 1, Imre Nagy was only repeating what every newspaper, leaflet, speech and broadcast proclaimed: "The revolutionary struggle fought by the Hungarian people and its heroes has at last carried the cause of freedom and independence to victory. . . . Working millions of Hungary, protect and strengthen *free, independent, democratic and neutral Hungary.*"

On November 3, Radio Free Kossuth summed up: "The over-whelming weight of Hungarian public opinion sees the result of the revolution as the establishment of a neutral, independent and democratic country, and just as it was ready to sweep out Stalinist tyranny, so it will protect with the same determination and firmness its regained democratic achievement."

The results of the general strike and the fighting had left industry almost at a standstill, with many factories smashed by shellfire. At first many workers were unwilling to return to their jobs until the Russians had completely left the country. But essential services were put into operation.

Thousands of young Freedom Fighters, most of them students or workers, still had arms in hand. They kept a discipline that has seldom been seen under such conditions. There was no looting, then, before or after. Some shooting was still occasionally heard. A few reprisals were carried out against some of the best known and most vicious of the A.V.H. agents. This is what the Communist propagandists now call "the White Terror," in their attempt to justify the unprovoked Russian attack. The A.V.H. agents were the torturers, jailers, murderers and betrayers of the families and friends of the young patriots. The A.V.H. was plotting

157

with the Russians to destroy Hungary's new freedom. With a regular police and courts not yet working, it is not hard to see why some of our young people took things into their own hands. By November 3 these incidents were coming to an end.

What is more surprising under the conditions is that the reprisals went no further. It was only the most notorious of the A.V.H. agents who were in danger. No violence was done to Communists, even to the Communists who had been the most pro-Russian, and the harshest supporters of the old Stalinist regime.

The confidence of the Freedom Fighters in the Nagy government was strengthened when their heroic commander, Pal Maleter, was made a Major General, and then brought into the Cabinet as Minister of Defense. They remembered how Maleter had personally held back the Russians in their onslaught on the Kilian barracks by backing his own tank into the only entranceway.

In an interview with Western journalists, Maleter told the story of the Freedom Revolution:

"This revolution was not organized by anybody. The revolution broke out because the Hungarian people wanted peace, tranquillity, freedom and independence, to which the foreign occupiers replied with weapons. At the beginning of the struggle, single groups, independent of each other, attacked the intruders without any sort of weapons and achieved their success with the weapons thus obtained. Hungarian youth made its own weapons."

In those four days of freedom, political liberty came

. . . Maleter had personally held back the Russians in their onslaught on the Kilian barracks by backing his own tank into the only entranceway.

quickly to life. The parties of the people, all united in the goal of an independent, free and neutral Hungary, set up their offices and brought out their newspapers. The Smallholders, Peasants, and Social Democrats all had leaders in the government. The Peasant Party changed its name to the Petofi Party, in honor of the great poet of Hungarian freedom. Even the Communist Party dropped its hated title, and called itself the Socialist Workers Party.

Before October 23 there had been only five newspapers in Budapest, all under complete Communist control. On November 4 there were twenty-five. Neither news nor opinions could be suppressed any longer.

Plans for a free general election were speeded.

Religious freedom, like political freedom, came back to strong life in those four days. Cardinal Mindszenty was back in Budapest, and spoke movingly to his people: "We, in our extremely grave situation, hope that we have no enemies, for we are the enemies of no one. We want to live in friendship with all people and all countries. . . . Now we need general elections, free from abuses, in which all parties can nominate candidates. The elections should be held under international supervision. . . . Personal revenge must be avoided and eliminated."

The Jewish rabbis and the revolutionary committee of the Jewish community broadcast: "Hungarian Jewry, having regained its religious freedom, enthusiastically salutes the achievements of the revolution, pays reverent homage to the heroes and identifies itself with the independent and free homeland."

The Presbyterians and Lutherans resumed public worship and activity. The Hungarian Presbyterian Church reappointed Bishop Laszlo Ravasz, who had been forced by the Communists to resign, as its leader.

The peasants resumed their winter plowing and sowing in the villages, and every day they sent food into Budapest. Compulsory food deliveries had been abolished—and at once there was more food. My wife, who lived in Budapest through those four days of freedom and the terrible days that followed, has told me how surprised she was at the amount of food that appeared in Budapest in those first days of November. The peasants were selling their produce now in a free market, and there was no profiteering.

It was lucky the food came. Everyone stocked their pantries. Otherwise they could never have gotten through the next ten days, when they had to huddle in the cellars as the Russian tanks smashed block after block of the city, and shot every human being who appeared on the street.

In the countryside, the peasants and their spokesmen were mapping the changes of the farm laws and regulations. All were agreed on the goal of a free farm economy based on the individual working farmers and peasants. Peasants would be free to join or leave the farm collectives. If the collectives were dissolved, the land, tools and stock were to be distributed to the individual peasants. Compulsory deliveries at government fixed prices were abolished.

The factory committees and workers' groups were putting forward the needs and demands of the workers, not the government. The right to strike—a criminal act under the

Communists—was upheld. Wages, prices, pension rights, working conditions were eagerly discussed and debated.

The economy was slowly getting on its feet. Everyone wanted to be on the streets together. What my wife later told me bears out the broadcast from Radio Free Kossuth that I heard in Vienna the evening of November 2:

"A picture of the streets in Budapest: Traffic is lively. Restaurants and coffee shops are all open. The newsboys shout twenty different newspaper headlines. There are more people in the streets than usual, for some of the workers are not yet back in the factories. The great thing is that more and more factories are starting work. One after the other, the great plants—Ganz, Lang, etc.—announce that they have started up. Streetcars are already running."

When I telephoned my wife on November 3, she told me these things, and spoke of "the joy" that the people felt. There was both sorrow and joy in their hearts. On All Souls' Night, November 1, every citizen of Budapest lighted a candle (as is our Hungarian custom) in his window, and this time carried another candle into the streets. The candles were for the souls of the city's dead heroes. They burned in the grey November night as Radio Free Kossuth broadcast the Requiem Mass of Mozart.

But the Russian forces had not left our country. On the contrary. More and more reports declared that Russian tanks and artillery were pouring across the border. Their armored units were spreading along the border next to Austria, in position to cut Hungary off from the West. Their tanks surrounded the airfields, pretending to "safeguard the evacuation." They were taking posts at railway stations, railway junctions and crossroads.

Moscow's spokesmen were lying in their customary manner. At the Kremlin and at the United Nations they denounced as "lies" and "slanders" all reports that the Russian troops in Hungary were being reinforced, or that there was any plan to resume hostilities. Soviet Russian Foreign Minister Shepilov fiercely repeated these denials on November 3.

The Hungarian government knew the Russian buildup was continuing. Imre Nagy had officially informed the United Nations that Hungary, withdrawing from the Warsaw Pact, declared itself a neutral country. He now informed the U.N. that new "Soviet military formations have crossed the country's frontier. . . . They are advancing toward Budapest." He appealed to the U.N. and the great powers to recognize and guarantee Hungary's neutrality.

Return of the Russians

At dawn on November 4, 1956, Soviet Russia attacked Hungary with 6,000 tanks, thousands of guns and armored cars, squadrons of light bombers, 200,000 soldiers—and a tidal wave of lies.

At 5:20 A.M. Imre Nagy made the following announcement over Radio Free Kossuth:

"This is Premier Imre Nagy speaking. Today at daybreak Soviet troops attacked our capital with the obvious intent of overthrowing the legal democratic Hungarian govern-

At dawn on November 4, 1956, Soviet Russia attacked Hungary with 6,000 tanks, thousands of guns and armored cars, squadrons of light bombers, 200,000 soldiers—and a tidal wave of lies.

ment. Our troops are in combat. The government is at its post. I notify the people of our country and the entire world of this fact."

This announcement was then repeated in English, Russian, Hungarian and French.

. At 8:00 A.M. Radio Free Kossuth broadcast the manifesto of the Union of Hungarian Writers:

"This is the Union of Hungarian Writers. To every writer in the world, to all scientists, to all writers' federations, to all science academies and associations, to the intelligentsia of the world! We ask all of you for help and support; there is but little time! You know the facts, there is no need to give you a special report! Help Hungary! Help the Hungarian writers, scientists, workers, peasants, and our intelligentsia!

"Help! Help! Help!

"S-O-S! S-O-S! S-O-S!"

Radio Free Kossuth then went out of existence. For nine hours there was no transmission from the station. At five o'clock it resumed broadcasting, under Russian control. At six o'clock it announced the formation of an illegal puppet government with Janos Kadar, the Communist Party Secretary, as Premier.

The exact details of what had happened are not known. The preceding night Pal Maleter and a colleague had been sent to negotiate with the Russian commander on the promised withdrawal. The Russians added one more piece of treachery to their list. They arrested and imprisoned the two envoys.

Their forces moved toward Budapest during the night of November 3/4. Nagy, in the Parliament Building, learned of the military attack, and prepared his brief broadcast announcement. Warned that Red Army troops were about to reach and capture him, he managed to escape and find refuge at the Yugoslav Embassy, along with about fifty others.*

Janos Kadar was still in the Parliament Building, it is said, when the Russians arrived. They ordered him to proclaim himself Premier, but Kadar at first refused. What pressures they applied, no one knows, but in the end, Kadar proved a coward and a traitor. He agreed to the shameful job of Moscow's puppet in the Russian Communist conquest and occupation of our country.

Throughout Hungary the Russian forces took over the railway stations, airfields, junctions, bridges, railway yards where they had already been posted. Their paratroops landed near Gyor. They struck at Szekesfehervar, Dunafoldvar, Veszprem and Sopron. At Pecs Hungarian troops, Freedom Fighters and workers, fought to guard the uranium mines against the Russian attack. At Tatabanya, miners and Hungarian soldiers smashed the railway line along which Red Army reinforcements were moving. More Russian armored units moved in from Czechoslovakia. Hungarian planes bombed the Russian pontoon bridges built across the Tisza river.

* On November 22 they left the Embassy under a safe conduct guarantee issued by Kadar. Continuing the record of treachery, Red Army troops seized them, and are said to have taken them to Rumania.

166

·The free radios broadcast their defiance: "Hungarian soldiers are fighting as one man against the invaders. The situation is serious but not hopeless. The fight against the intruder is raging everywhere. Hungarians, do not let Russian troops carry out a massacre in our beloved country! Take your arms and stand united for the sacred cause of the defense of the country! Death to the Soviet occupiers!"

But a direct military struggle of the ten million Hungarians against the Soviet Russian giant could not last for long. On the afternoon of November 4 tragic words were heard from the voice of a free station:

"Civilized people of the world, listen and come to our aid, not with declarations, but with force, with soldiers and arms. Do not forget that there is no stopping the wild onslaught of Bolshevism. Your turn will also come, once we perish. Save our souls! Save our souls!

"Peoples of Europe whom we helped for centuries to withstand the barbaric attacks. . . . listen to the tolling of Hungarian bells warning against disaster. . . . Civilized people of the world, we implore you to help us in the name of justice, of freedom, of the binding moral principle of active solidarity. Our ship is sinking. Light is failing, the shadows grow darker every hour over the soil of Hungary. Listen to the cry, civilized peoples of the world, and act; extend to us your fraternal hand.

"S-O-S! S-O-S!—May God be with you."

But one after the other the free radio voices were replaced by the voice of the Russian command. The changed control of the radio stations marked the progress of the

Russian arms. On the 4th, Radio Szombathely fell. On the 5th, we heard Radio Free Szolnok for the last time. On the night of the 5th, the Soviet Russian military commander began issuing his orders over Radio Pecs. Radio Gyor was in Russian hands by the 7th.

On the 7th and 8th, Radio Free Rakoczi broadcast its last reports and appeals:

"In the name of all honest Hungarians we appeal to all honest men in the world.

"Do you love liberty? So do we.

"Do you have wives and children? So do we. And what shall we give to our children who are asking for bread? The last piece of bread has been eaten.

"The U.N. is able to stop further bloodshed. Or shall we lose faith in the conscience and decency of the world when we are fighting for world freedom?

"We ask you to repeat in Russian the following appeal to Soviet soldiers in Hungary:

"Soldiers!

"Why do you want to crush our liberty? You can see that it is not factory proprietors, not landowners, and not the bourgeoisie who have taken up arms against you, but the Hungarian people, who are fighting desperately.

"Soldiers! Do not take up arms against the Hungarian nation!"

But by November 9 the voices of Hungarian freedom had left the air. There was only silence, the Russian commands and Communist lies.

For a week the ferocious fighting continued. Our heroes

chose death instead of the loss of freedom. The fighting went on in Dunapentele, Gyor, Pecs, Komlo, and in Budapest and its suburbs.

The Russian guns fired on anything that moved: Red Cross trucks, school children, bread lines, a face at a window. But the Red troops were still afraid. In Budapest a tank did not dare go alone along a street, and they still moved out at night from the narrower streets.

The civilian population of Budapest waited in the cellars as the guns destroyed the houses and buildings above them. The Freedom Fighters, the Hungarian army and the workers continued fierce resistance for a week. They fought in small groups from the houses and alleys. They would attack a tank or gun, and then escape quickly through underground passages and the backs of buildings.

In some of the big buildings, and in the factories of the working-class sections the fighting was on a bigger scale. Thousands of workers and young Freedom Fighters were barricaded in the giant Csepel steel plant and in the factories of Ujpest on the north of the city. In Budapest, as in the industrial areas of Sztalinvaros and Pecs, it was the working-class districts that held out longest.

While the Russian guns were killing our people and destroying our cities, their lies were aimed at our souls and at the whole world. Kadar and his fellow-traitors followed the orders of his Russian masters. Their broadcasts and newspapers spread the lie that our Freedom Revolution—the revolution of the entire Hungarian nation except for a handful of fanatics and traitors and Russian agents—was a

169

For tens of thousands, the only course was refuge in the free world.

plot by fascists, counter-revolutionists, Western agents and Nazis.

And they spread the lie that Kadar and his dozen Russian puppets are "the government of Hungary."

No Hungarian believes any of their lies. Can they make the world believe them?

Hungary Will Be Free

By November 10 large scale fighting ended. A few strong resistance points held out for several days more. Guerrilla and partisan actions go on, and have kept breaking out ever since.

The Hungarian people did not surrender. Their Freedom Revolution did not suffer a total defeat. There has been no counter-revolution. What has happened is this. A foreign imperialist aggressor—The Soviet Union—invaded our country with overwhelming military strength. In a week-long battle he won a military victory in the field. He rules Hungary for the time being by military occupation. He makes use of a puppet government—the government of Kadar—that is rejected by the whole nation as a fraud.

Hungary was alone. The U.N. and the governments of the free world had not answered Hungary's appeals. Unaided, it was impossible for the Hungarians to continue a massive open military struggle against the invader. For tens of thousands, the only course was refuge in the free world.

Yet in the free world, while governments debated courses of action, the people of the free world rose up, in horror

Yet in the free world, while governments debated courses of action, the people rose up, in horror and anger. . . .

and anger at the brutal use of Communist tanks and troops to put down the Hungarian Freedom Revolution. Workers and students marched in sympathy demonstrations for the repressed Hungarian patriots, or stood silent to honor the dead. Soviet Russian embassies in free world capitals were stoned; Communist publishing houses were set afire. Flags flew at half-mast in many cities.

In London, the marching crowds wore black arm-bands to mourn those who gave their lives to free Hungary from Russian control. The entire population of Denmark stood in silence for five minutes, while church bells tolled. In Bogota, Hungarian citizens living in Colombia, dressed in costumes of their homeland, staged a public demonstration demanding the withdrawal of Red Army troops from Hungary and expulsion of the Soviet Union from the United Nations. In Santa Ana, El Salvador, thousands of citizens silently marched through the streets carrying lighted candles. Bells of the city tolled for hours. The procession ended at the Cathedral, where a solemn requiem mass was sung. In West Germany, flags flew at half-mast for three days.

In Rome, Paris, Saigon, Madrid, Lisbon and Geneva, students marched in the streets, carrying slogans condemning Russian aggression in Hungary. In the United States churches and synagogues offered special prayers for the Hungarian people, and college and university students held protest meetings.

Free labor groups all over the world registered their dismay at the brutal Communist oppression of the people

Free men everywhere showed that they are determined to make the cause of Free Hungary their own.

of Hungary. Work stoppages to show sympathy with the Hungarian people took place in Belgium, Denmark, France, West Germany, Greece, Italy, Korea, Malta, the Netherlands, Pakistan, the Philippines, Thailand, Tunisia and various countries in the Caribbean area.

The British Trade Union Congress advised its affiliated unions to "abandon any plans they might have for exchange visits to the Soviet Union." The Executive Board of the Swedish Trade Union Federation issued a resolution denouncing "the terror by which the Hungarian dictatorship, supported by Russian arms, has sought to crush the Hungarian nation's heroic fight for democratic freedom and national independence."

Free men everywhere showed that they are determined to make the cause of Free Hungary their own.

Meanwhile the Freedom Revolution nurses its wounds and gathers its strength. The fight goes on, but by other means: by passive resistance, strikes, pressures, defiance, boycotts, prayer, by peasants and workers, clerks and students and writers, children and mothers and old people— by the whole Hungarian nation.

Victory has been postponed, not lost!

Hungary will win her freedom! There is not power enough on earth to stop her!

ACKNOWLEDGEMENTS

Pictures on pages 24, 79, and 170 courtesy of United Press Association Newspictures; on pages 26, 64, and 69 courtesy of Wide World Photos, Inc.; on pages 53 and 54 courtesy of Peter Schmid: Pix, Inc.; on page 55, upper right, courtesy of the Giloon Agency; on pages 71 and 164 courtesy of Black Star Publishing Co.; on page 122 courtesy of Magnum Photos, Inc.; on page 131 courtesy of Acme Newspictures; on page 172 (center, the Philip Murray Building) courtesy of *Washington Post*; on page 172 (upper right corner) Ampfoto, The Hague.